WISE WOMEN
OF THE
DREAMTIME

WISE WOMEN
OF THE
DREAMTIME

ABORIGINAL TALES
OF THE ANCESTRAL POWERS

Collected by K. Langloh Parker

Edited with Commentary by Johanna Lambert

Inner Traditions International
Rochester, Vermont

Inner Traditions International
One Park Street
Rochester, Vermont 05767
www.InnerTraditions.com

Library of Congress Cataloging-in-Publication Data

Wise women of the dreamtime: aboriginal tales of the ancestral powers/
   collected by K. Langloh Parker; edited with commentary by Johanna
   Lambert.
       p. cm.
   Includes bibliographical references.
   ISBN 0-89281-477-2
   1. Australian aborigines—Folklore. 2. Mythology, Australian
aboriginal.   I. Parker, K. Langloh (Katie Langloh), 1856-1940.
II. Lambert, Johanna.
GR371.4.A87W57   1993
398.2'0899915—dc20   93-377
                                   CIP

Printed and bound in the United States

10 9

Text design by Bonnie Atwater
This book was typeset in Optima with Lithos as a display typeface

This book is dedicated to the re-imagining and re-dreaming of the existence of a harmonious relationship between humanity and all of the natural world. Just as Aboriginal women are the gatherers of the plants and the seeds, now is the time for the potencies of the Universal Feminine to be re-gathered, re-remembered with the traditional Aboriginal culture as a guiding force.

CONTENTS

Acknowledgments   ix

Preface   xi

Introduction   1

· TALES OF THE ANCESTRAL POWERS ·

Wahwee and Nerida: The Water Monster and the Water Lily   18

Dinewan the Man Changes to Dinewan the Emu   28

Sturt's Desert Pea, the Blood Flower   33

Where the Frost Comes From   44

· TALES OF THE ANIMAL POWERS ·

Murgah Muggui, the Spider   54

Bralgah, the Dancing Bird   61

Piggiebillah, the Porcupine   71

The Rainbird   80

· TALES OF THE MAGICAL POWERS ·

Moodoobahngul, the Widow   90

The Wirreenun Woman and Her Wirreenun Son   96

The Redbreasts   104

The Wagtail and the Rainbow   111

· TALES OF HEALING ·

Goonur, the Woman-Doctor   118

The Bunbundoolooeys   134

Bibliography   144

ACKNOWLEDGMENTS

My initial appreciation I extend to the Aboriginal people and culture, the understanding of which has opened a new door on my perception of life.

To Brian Syron, my Aboriginal teacher and friend, I give thanks for his unusual ability to communicate the craft of acting and for his penetrating insight into universal symbology.

Aboriginal women who have influenced and helped shape my imagination of the feminine in Aboriginal culture in a myriad of ways are: Stella Mankara, Bell McLeod, Lydia Miller, Rosalie Graham, and Leslie Fogarty. I thank them all for their inspiration.

I am most appreciative to Aboriginal artist Dorothy Djukulul for permission to reproduce her bark paintings. The simple power of her abstract compositions, combined with her skillful artistry, captures the living essence of the animal species and, therefore, the Aboriginal Ancestors she portrays. My thanks to Elaine Kitchener, the photographer of Dorothy's work, for all her efforts and time.

Also I am very grateful to Marcie Muir, whose skillful and insightful book, *My Bush Book,* based on the life of K. Langloh Parker, was invaluable.

To the publisher, Ehud Sperling, I am appreciative for the confidence he placed in my ability to express the value of these most archaic legends. I am grateful to Estella Arias for her personal support and for giving so generously her aesthetic concern in the visual presentation of this book. I offer many thanks to the editorial staff at Inner Traditions, particularly to Leslie Colket and Lee Wood, who were amiable and unwavering in their support. To copyeditor Jill Mason and to Bonnie Atwater and Jeanie Levitan, please accept my appreciation for your skillful and creative work.

I also wish to thank Jeanne Bultman for her many hours of fastidious and corrective readings as well as her warm encouragement.

To my love, Robert Lawlor, I am indebted for not only his unwavering support and his bountiful reserve of spirit, ideas, and knowledge, but also his awe and respect of the earth, the Universal Feminine—its beauty as well as its dark and hidden powers. The final two commentaries, in particular, resulted from a complete and balanced male/female collaboration.

PREFACE

On a steaming summer's day in February 1862, six-year-old Katie Langloh Parker (then Katie Field), with her two sisters and a beautiful young Aboriginal girl, Miola, ventured down to the Darling River. As they did often in the searing heat of Australian outback summers, the young girls stripped to their bathers to swim and frolic in the soothing waters. However, the beauty and innocence of this moment crystallized into a staggering event that changed Katie's life and sensibilities forever and triggered reverberations, in European awareness, of the heart and spirit of the world's oldest culture—the Australian Aborigines.

Katie and her younger sister, the first two to slip into the water, unknowingly ventured beyond secure depths. Suddenly, the bucolic atmosphere, ringing with youthful feminine laughter, was transformed into one of terror and chaos. Gripped by panic, the two girls began screaming for assistance. Miola, who had remained on the bank, plunged into the waters to rescue Katie, while the older Field sister swam to the aid of the youngest. Once Miola had made sure Katie was safe, she immediately began running and yelling for help, crying, "Save the girls from the wild blacks!" This strange and fateful phrasing grew out of the Aboriginal belief that drownings were caused by "wild spirit blacks" who dragged unwitting victims down to their deep abode.

Katie's pioneer father heard Miola, but he believed she was warning him of an attack on the homestead by some "wild" Aborigines. As he prepared for a tribal assault, the possibility of rescue slipped into the tide of lost moments. When he finally arrived at the river both of Katie's sisters had drowned.[1]

Many years later, when asked by her new husband if she was frightened to move with him from the city to his remote sheep property in the "Never Never" land of the Australian outback, Katie unhesitatingly responded, "How can I be frightened of the Aborigines? It is these people to whom I owe my life."[2]

When she survived the childhood drowning episode, her imaginal core had been drawn forever into the depths of Aboriginal culture. It was the mind, life, and spirit of these people in which she found stimulation and inspiration and toward whom she would dedicate her lifelong intellectual and literary involvement. She was instinctively regarded by Aboriginal people as a trusted friend, and she was among the earliest to whom they disclosed their legends.[3]

Being by nature a curious and skilled observer, Katie Parker was intrigued and respectful of the strange myths, elaborate ceremonies, and secret culture of the Aborigines. She was given access to the ceremonies and practices of Aboriginal women from which male anthropologists were, for the most part, excluded.

Without academic education or motivation, Parker gathered, translated, and published a considerable collection of Aboriginal myths and factual depictions of Aboriginal customs. A vast number of the stories were told to her by Aboriginal friends who lived or worked near, or on, her husband's extensive sheep property. The complex process she chose for translation illustrates her dedication to accuracy and fidelity: The story was repeated to her a number of times by the storyteller in the presence of a bilingual intermediary. She would then read back her translation, allowing the storyteller to check the translated meaning of each word as well as corroborating the thrust and concept of the story.[4] Consequently, these renditions breathe life into our experience of Aboriginal legends, which, for the most part, have been handled in the sterile terminology of the androcentric world of British anthropology. The legends did not in any way gain from Parker's translations into English; on the contrary, she stressed that in the process of fixing an oral tradition in the confines of written words, the subtle, intimate, and diatonic animation of the storyteller, and all that was conveyed through a living presence, was irretrievably lost.[5]

Her publications were received enthusiastically in London and America. In Australia, however, the reception was much more subdued. A few Australian anthropologists credited her diligent work, but more generally the legends were regarded as childish in nature and the Aboriginal culture inconsequential. One such review in the *Bulletin* of January 9, 1896, claimed that the tales had "ethnologically little significance . . . , that *this group of Aborigines* are evidently as happy in thoughtlessness as all their kindred. . . . The undoubted value of the collection is chiefly that of a literary curiosity—the prattlings of our Australia's children, which even in their worthlessness must have charm for a parent."[6] Such was the backdrop of widespread bigotry and ignorance concerning the Aboriginal culture that existed in Australia during Parker's lifetime and that, surprisingly, is still prevalent.

Parker's life was underscored by the great sorrow of witnessing the Aboriginal people fade from their beloved lands as the merciless procession of colonialization continued across Australia. Her life's work grew out of the ironic tragedy of belonging to, and in every way being a part of, the colonialism that destroyed the very people to whom she was indebted and in whom she had discovered such beauty and depth of spirituality.

The spiritual, sexual, and emotional freedom of the Aborigines stirred inner conflicts with Parker's Christian Victorian upbringing. Her inward identity with Aboriginal culture danced against the backdrop of her Anglo-Saxon conditioning and revealed itself by several inconsistencies in the perspective of her research. Understandably, she was unable to fully value Aboriginal polytheistic animism, which viewed every creature and aspect of nature as a spiritual reflection of the great Ancestral Beings that brought the earth into existence. Like almost all Western scholars of the time, she could conceive of religion only in the narrow criteria of monotheism, the belief in one all-powerful male god, which alone was used to designate whether a culture was "civilized." Her Christian conditioning was probably responsible for her attempts to equate one of the powerful male Ancestral Beings, described in the myths as Biame, with the Christian Father God.

By superimposing monotheism on the Aborigines, she attempted to bypass the Darwinian label of "primitive" and present the depth of their spirituality and perception to the Western world. On the other hand, she contradicted the prevailing androcentric views, in that she emphasized the feminine in her collection of myths and also regarded Biame's wife, Birrahgnooloo, as the "Mother of all life."[7] In this sense, her role can be viewed as a very early step in unmasking the domination of Western scholarship and science by a rational, male, sky-hero, father-son belief system, as well as a vital link to the more ancient, earth-honoring, feminine-based spirituality. Within the last decade several female anthropologists have conducted comprehensive studies on the role of women in Aboriginal society and brought new awareness of their autonomy, the extensiveness of their rituals and ceremonies, and their role as healers. However, long before this broadening of academic understanding, Parker recognized connections between the ancient Aboriginal myths and actual incidents of magic that she witnessed.

Parker's exposure to the occult world of feminine sorcery occurred, for the most part, through her close Aboriginal friend Bootha. Well over sixty years of age, Bootha developed her healing and magical powers after the tragic death of her granddaughter. In despair she isolated herself, speaking to no one, and exhibited behavior that Parker regarded at first as lunacy. The Aborigines, on the other hand, interpreted Bootha's behavior as a process of becoming "spirit possessed." After a period of severe illness, Bootha emerged rejuvenated, with magical powers to heal, communicate with the spirits, and "make" rain.[8] Parker recounts a number of situations when Bootha successfully brought rain to her drought-ridden gardens.[9] One wonders how often cases of mental illness, emotional withdrawal, or volatility in our society are, in reality, a passage into occult dimensions of awareness.

Bootha also healed a young friend of Parker's who became mysteriously ill and lay bedridden. Parker watched in a skeptical manner as Bootha contacted her spirit helpers, who arrived as gushes of wind and spoke in whispering voices. One of these spirits informed Bootha that the source of illness was not physical but psychic. The old woman saw in a vision that the young girl had inadvertently insulted the spirits of a particular sacred tree and had been attacked by invisible bees. This explained huge welts on the girl's back that she had kept hidden from everyone including Parker. With Bootha's remedies, she was cured overnight, and Parker's and her friend's skepticism was replaced with amazement.[10]

In the ancient way of being, the earth not only creates, feeds, and protects life but, like a mother, whispers through natural signs and images the secret knowledge of how body, mind, emotions, and spirit work upon each other in an intricate, invisible weaving. From this weaving Aboriginal people were able to blend deep psychic powers with human societal law and with all the energies embedded in the creations and creatures of nature. Katie Langloh Parker's life and work is a very early footbridge arching over a vast cultural chasm, the lost memory of humanity's tribal heritage. It carries us across to a time when a mysterious feminine science of life, love, and healing was envisioned by ancient storytellers. Their tales were drawn from a contemplative listening to the shadows of leaves, to the flight and song of birds, to the scurry and prance of animals, to the cry of the wind and night owl.

Aboriginal women, in addition to their exclusive ceremonies, explained the origins and destiny of humanity through the art of storytelling and, by this means, molded the enduring values and dynamics of tribal life. In this collection of legends we are able to view women as the central characters, providing a view of the deep magical feminine and preformative powers as they roamed the earth and they created the natural world during the great

Dreamtime epoch. Throughout, the feminine emerges as a mighty co-conspirator in the setting of the Dreamtime stage and the structure of the ancestral realms.

These archaic Dreamtime legends were rescued from drowning in the dark tide of colonialism and patriarchal progress by a brilliant, courageous woman. In these legends we are allowed to remember the joy and profundity of life harmonized again within the mysteries of the Universal Feminine and her great dreaming—the natural world.

ENDNOTES

1. Marcie Muir, *My Bush Book: K. Langloh Parker's 1890's Story of the Outback Station Life* (Sydney: Rigby Publishers, 1982), 25.
2. Ibid., 46.
3. K. Langloh Parker, *Australian Legendary Tales*, edited by H. Drake Brockman (Sydney: Angus and Robertson, 1974), vi.
4. Muir, *My Bush Book*, 173.
5. Ibid.
6. Ibid, 171.
7. K. Langloh Parker, *The Euahlayi Tribe: A Study of Aboriginal Life in Australia*, (London: Constable, 1905), 7.
8. Ibid., 42.
9. Ibid., 44–46.
10. Ibid., 48.

INTRODUCTION

The melodic warbling of the magpies and the raucous, gurgling laugh of the kookaburras perched in the silver-gray foliage of the eucalyptus heralded the arrival of many of my childhood days and filled me then, as they do now, with the enchantment that is particular to the Australian bush. Also etched in my memory are the sultry pink clouds of evening dusted with thousands of black wings as flying foxes squawked their way into the twilight. Birds and animals and the haunting, timeless presence of the bush played a major part in my life and my dreams from an early age.

When I came upon the Aboriginal legends collected by K. Langloh Parker, the mythic and poetic dimensions of the native fauna and flora, which embodied the spiritual core of Australia's "first born," found a prepared passage into my imagination. This affinity with the Aboriginal culture, which I discovered in my childhood response to nature, continues to grow with my involvement and encounters with Aboriginal people, their way of life, their myths and stories, and their contemporary struggles. Both the vast depth in their dark and ancient eyes and the boundless spaciousness of the Australian landscape reflect the unfathomable history their culture encompasses. Aboriginal women, in particular, evoke a sense of inner strength, compassion, and knowing that has acted as the backbone in the preservation of their culture through the near genocide of oppression, disease, and alcoholism during the last two hundred years of European colonization. I believe the source of this inner strength is portrayed by the female Ancestors, such as those depicted in this collection of stories, who encompass the full spectrum, the darkness and the light, of feminine qualities and characteristics.

An event that captures for me like a still photograph the openness and power of Aboriginal women was my brief friendship with Stella, a woman from the Tiwi people who live on Bathurst Island off the coast of Northern Australia. My companion and I had been invited to attend a traditional Aboriginal funeral ceremony in which there was much dancing, wailing, and singing. At one point I turned from the dance, and my eyes fixed upon a slender, dark body clad in a threadworn floral frock. Almost like an apparition, this smiling face with thick silver hair moved in my direction, and Stella then sat in a graceful swirl next to me. She was over seventy years of age, her knee was bandaged, and she walked with a hobble, yet nothing could deter her from intermittently entering into the dance. During her breaks she began to inform me of the symbolic roles and familial relationships of the various people in the ceremony. As she smoked her crab-claw pipe, she talked at length of her culture, her family, and her fond memories of "bush life" prior to the rule of the Catholic mission. Her animated chatter ranged from bursts of warm laughter to serious and compelling sentiment. With joy and assurance, her thought and conversation danced openly between her dreams, her intimate feelings, and deeper insights and details of the joys and struggles of her ordinary life. She did not possess the polite guardedness and formality that one often encounters in relating to older generations in our society. Although we were together only a short time, we wept when saying goodbye.

Every researched indigenous culture makes reference to the primary polarities or complementations of opposites that are evident in the natural world, such as night/day, moist/dry, expansion/contraction. These have been variously named All-Mother/All-Father, Moon/Sun, Earth/Sky, and Yin/Yang. This philosophical and linguistic structure has been absorbed into our traditional philosophies—Greek mythology, European alchemy, and the teachings of Pythagoras. The opposites have also been dominant in Hindu metaphysics as Prakiti/Purusha and in Egyptian cosmology as Isis/Osiris. In all of these age-old traditions, certain characteristics are allotted to each of the achetypal polarities, which are considered the Universal Masculine and Universal Feminine. This philosophy of universal polarity has more recently been continued in the works of Emma Jung, Carl Jung, Marion Woodman, and Joseph Campbell.

Traditional Aboriginal society is founded on the preeminence of the characteristics of the Universal Feminine, epitomized by its unwavering respect for the earth, which Aborigines refer to as "the mother."[1] Their social order encourages, from infancy, empathetic concern and compassion toward all creatures of nature, as well as deep loyalties and responsibilities to their kin and the group as a whole. While these feminine characteristics are paramount, they do not translate into power-based hierarchical social structures as have the excessive masculine qualities within our patriarchal society. Within the Universal Feminine qualities such as receptivity, mutability, interrelatedness, and diffusion that are predominant in Aboriginal society, the creative Universal Masculine characteristics such as limitation, order, structure, and definition also find balanced expression.

Poet and law woman Daisy Utemorra, of the Wandjina people, an elder of the Kimberley tribes of Western Australia, related in a conversation that after men have obtained the highest degrees of male initiation "only then do they become eligible for initiation into women's law." Recognition of the feminine basis of this earliest hunting and gathering society lends support to the theories of the renowned anthropologist Marija Gimbutas, who has explored the transition from prehistoric to historic in terms of an alternation between matriarchal, or feminine, preeminence and patriarchy, or masculine domination.[2] One of the most ancient Dreamtime stories, "Djankawu," indicates such a historical pattern. In this story the two sisters of Djankawu discover that their brother has stolen their dilly bags full of emblems of power and sacred ritual. The older sister considers that it may be time for them to relinquish their power and allow the men, for a period, to take control by possessing the sacred bag. The sisters understand that as women the knowledge is innate within them and that, besides, they have their uteruses, which hold not the symbolic but the actual power of creation.[3]

It is in the context of such historical ideas that I find the importance of bringing forth these legends pertaining to the forces and characteristics of the feminine within the Aboriginal worldview. With the power and influence of women rising significantly over the last twenty or more years, these interpretations of the feminine, taken from the earliest of human cultures, are of contemporary significance.

My preparation for exploring these legends has not been academic anthropology but rather my long friendship and association with the Aboriginal film and theater director and drama teacher Brian Syron. Mr. Syron brought to the examination of Western dramatic literature a deeply symbolic vision, which he seemed to draw from the archaic depths of his native culture. He worked with an intuitive sense that symbols resound through the transparency of time and that a symbolic essence or relationship found in a Dreamtime story can be equally discovered in a play by Shakespeare or Chekhov. I have based my interpretation of these stories, from a purely oral tradition, in the spirit that their symbolic material is "alive," transforming in time, viewable in a multiplicity of ways, and with meanings that do not deny one other. It is this ancient voice of storytelling that affected K. Langloh Parker.

An avid reader, Parker developed a passion for European literature at a young age and became well versed in ancient mythologies, particularly Greek.[4] This early initiation into universal symbology formed the ground of understanding and openmindedness from which she recognized the significance, beauty, and sophistication of the Aboriginal legends. In her writings, she noted that parallels and symbolic connections might exist between the vastly older Dreamtime stories and the mythologies of more recent cultures;[5] however, she did not pursue this theory. In this book I intend to follow her insight and interpret her translations comparatively with other world mythologies.

Ten thousand years ago, all of our beginnings sprang from the cultural well of hunting and gathering. This book is a personal, philosophical, and psychological exploration of certain aspects of the traditional Australian Aborigines. The spirit of this traditional culture and some of the practices are alive in many Aboriginal people today, reverberating in the landforms and animals of this most ancient continent. Therefore, I have used the present tense throughout these commentaries; the spirit of the culture which I am attempting to evoke is eternal.

I have not wished to appropriate information nor speak for the Aboriginal people: rather, this book has been an imaginal voyage. By absorbing my thought in their mythology and contemplating their way of life, it has been possible to redream their archaic presence on this land.

I hope that my glimpse into the stories of this ancient culture will serve as a brief contour of the symbolic depth of a society grounded in humanity's original perception. Although antiquity of the Aborigines is academically disputed—estimates range from 40,000 to 150,000 years—by either the most conservative or the most liberal chronological dating, the Aboriginal people are indisputably the oldest continuous culture on earth.[6]

Dreamtime stories are the predecessors of what we have come to call myths. In a sense, they encompass all of the definitions and functions that have been attributed or pinned to the word *myth* throughout history. The origin of *myth* lies in the Greek concept of *mythos:* archetypal themes and psychic and psychological realities upon which cultural beliefs or patterns of behavior are based. In contemporary times this concept has been displaced by the idea of fictitious tales with invented characters and events. Dreamtime stories are myths when one considers the mythic process as a mode of perceiving, experiencing, and expressing the relationships between our visible world and the invisible forces, patterns, and intelligences that have existed since before the world's creation. Contemporary scientific "cosmology of creation" models vast fields of gravity and electromagnetism as the forces of attraction and repulsion that were causative in the formation of the material universe. These fields of force continue to affect every aspect of that creation while remaining virtually incomprehensible, invisible influences. Such forces are comparable, in many ways, to the mythological or Dreamtime concept of a priori metaphysical beings whose interractions and interrelationship brought the natural world into existence and who continue to affect all of life as invisible patterns and energies.

Originally, myths, or Dreamtime stories, were not expressed simply in verbal or written form but were enacted, chanted, painted, costumed, danced, sung, and imagined, sometimes in deep hypnotic and hallucinatory states. In this manner the creative energies and relationships hidden beneath the natural world were brought into the conscious realm. The mythic process was believed to create a continuous chain from the metaphysical phase (the Dreamtime) through to the natural creation. Flowing from this original creation, the same principles and relationships are imprinted in life as in the fundamental human relationships into which we are all born. In this way, nature and human society are considered to have a common source.

In contemporary times myth is synonymous with the word *legend,* reflecting another Greek word, *legein,* or *logos.* This word contains such meanings as "word," "light," "language," and "law." In a wider sense, it refers to the entire process of representing the principles of order and interrelationship from one level of existence to another. Mythos/logos is the activity of consciousness that transfers the underlying forms and powers from the unconscious to the conscious, from the metaphysical to the physical, from nature to society, from energetic to substantial, from symbol to reality.

In presenting these stories I am attempting to catch a glimpse of how a society allows its laws and various levels of initiatic knowledge to flow from metaphysical dimensions and the realms of the deep subjective unconscious. Its social laws enabled Aboriginal culture to flourish for perhaps 100,000 years or more. The continuation of the Aborigines' "Dreamtime law" is assured by the constancy of ritual and ceremonial life in which they enter into ecstatic or trance states, contacting and listening to the voices of the Ancestors echoing from the great Dreamtime.

The contemporary world diverged from the original process of mythos/logos in attempting to create laws and language strictly from the rational conscious activities of the mind. Relegating mythos to a subjective and fictional status allows our behavioral codes and economic formats to be based solely on external arbitrary structures. Our laws, in opposition to the intrinsic patterns and forces of both nature and the unconscious, create kingdoms and governments that are perpetually being overthrown, destroyed, or replaced.

The Dreamtime, from which all societal law originated, can be described as a vast epoch that occurred, according to the Aborigines, "before time began." All the Dreamtime stories, or Aboriginal myths, depict events from the Dreamtime, which existed prior to the appearance of the manifest world. This was a period when great mythical powers and beings pervaded infinite space and, with almost incomprehensible intensity and force, lived out their dreams unencumbered by the limits and definitions of embodied existence. The entire contents of universal consciousness—every imaginable physical and psychological characteristic, interaction, and relationship—poured through the dramas of the Dreamtime creative Ancestors.[7]

The exploits and mode of being of the great Ancestors resonate, to a lesser degree, with our experience of dreaming. That is, during our dreams, space and time are unbounded. One's dreaming self floats in a world beyond the rational, where subject and object, meaning and form merge and separate kaleidoscopically. We find ourselves metamorphosing into other beings and them into us. In our dreams the qualities and characteristics of inner consciousness symbolize themselves, as did those of the great Ancestors, in human, animal, or plant form.

In Aboriginal cosmology the Dreamtime epoch concluded; however, the energy and vibrational patterns from the exploits of the great Ancestors congealed the initially limitless space into the topography and forms that we now experience as the material aspect of the universe. The land, its forms and features, as well as the subtle vibrational energy emanating from an earthly place, is the imprint or record of Dreamtime episodes. During the Dreamtime, the Ancestors could transform from humans to animals, until, at the conclusion of this world-creating epoch, they retired to their abode beneath the earth and in the sky. At that time, human and animal became distinct species. However, the emotional, psychological, and psychic characteristics of humans remained symbolized in the physical characteristics and behavior of the animals. Therefore, the Aboriginal worldview can be seen as founded upon a distinct twoness, or fundamental duality at the basis of creation: the Dreamtime epoch that occurred and has concluded, and the earthly creations, or physical reality, that emerged after the Dreaming.[8]

The myths that the Aborigines have transmitted for untold generations were conceived from visualizing what must have taken place in a particular region in order to have the earthly environment take on its shape and condition. Behavioral codes, or Dreaming laws, were subsequently laid down for human society based on this endless array of mythic events and their significance and outcomes. The original sense of mythos/logos differs from that which we inherited from the Greeks. In classical myths the Gods, or archetypes (Ancestors), have become generalized as universal influences associated with astrological configurations in the sky and supposedly with unchanging characteristics of a universal collective unconscious. In contrast, Aborigines associate these ancestral powers with specific land formations and natural features, and they do not consider their inner psychic landscape to be fixed by generalized collective archetypes. Rather, the Aborigines are inwardly transfigured by the vibrational energies intrinsic to the numerous sacred sites they travel to and from, and they manifest very different characters according to the role they play in the ceremony associated with a particular earthly place.[9]

To avoid psychological and social repression, the dark, excessive, utterly centric, or expansive and extreme, or destructive characteristics depicted in the stories were outlawed in society, yet freely expressed in colorful ceremonial enactment and dance. The Dreaming laws are derived from a sustained balance and harmony between the opposing forces that, as I have said, are a priori and inherent in the natural world. These forces—such as attraction and repulsion, interdependency and autonomy, contraction and expansion—are found within the dynamics of the human psyche and human relationships. As the historian Joseph Campbell pointed out in his classic work *The Hero with a Thousand Faces*, (Princeton University Press, 1973), much of mythology entails the process of balancing and harmonizing the universal forces that are reflected in the sets of relationships each person is involved with throughout life: father/daughter, mother/son, sister/brother, wife/husband, etc. These same familial patterns in the Chinese Book of Changes, the *I Ching,* again represent the universal principles of order. When one's familial or social relationships fail to reflect those of the metaphysical and natural world, the underlying ongoing powers of creation are prevented or blocked from sustaining humanity and nature, and a cycle of disharmony, disintegration, and destruction ensues.

It is this cosmology that prompted Aboriginal society to transfer from generation to generation the laws concerning marital patterns, familial respect, and responsibility codes as well as a strict ethic in regard to a metaphysical reality and a sacred earth. The rigorous taboos of familial relationships, physical and psychological, are based upon the belief that metaphysical laws are reflected in human relationship patterns. For example, in the natural world, cohesive enduring patterns are necessary to create form and substance. The tendency to endure and be everlasting replicates itself in human psychology in the desire to impose one's values and way of being onto the life of one's children and successive generations. If this tendency for fixation becomes excessive or imbalanced, it creates a stagnant, inverted, or incestuous atmosphere. Aboriginal society mitigated unconscious incestual projections by diverting familial attachment into establishing a kinship and continuous relationship with the wider sphere of nature, totems, and spiritual ancestry. Continuity and the drive for immortality that in our society rests in possession of familial lineage, ownership, and bequeathing of material wealth and power was, in the Aboriginal society, transferred to the continuation of a metaphysically derived culture of which each individual is an integral and enduring part.

The Aborigines explore the forces of fixed attachment, possession, ownership, personal power, and individual immortality in their Dreamtime enactments but remain a socio-centric culture nested in the delicately balanced ecology of the physical world. Each individual is foremost an intrinsic part of a group, one in which kin and clan members are considered as much a part of the self as one's own arms and legs. No Aboriginal language has possessive pronouns. For example: "my uncle" or "my brother" would be expressed "uncle me" or "brother me."[10] The sense of belonging to a group is so powerful in Aboriginal consciousness that when a person is isolated, for example during incarceration, he or she experiences such a devastating sense of incompleteness that sickness and sometimes death result.[11]

Another focus of attention in these Aboriginal Dreamtime stories is the complex, invisible, and concurrent relationship between a spirit existence and a bodily existence and, particularly, the separation of these two at death. Stories often depict the temporary disintegration of body-spirit relatedness, which is provoked in initiatic procedures and which allows for the possibility of rebirth of an individual within his or her lifetime. Death, the permanent loss of embodied consciousness and the subsequent disintegration of the body, is considered the greatest initiation rite of all. Initiation can be explained as the ritualization of death and rebirth, an experience that is essential to a full embracing of life and one that we seek either consciously or unconsciously in order to prepare for our inevitable final transition. For this preparation, Aboriginal men, at various initiatic stages, have elaborate formal ceremonies that include death enactments or deep unconscious trance experiences. Women, for the most part, undergo initiation through their natural processes of menstruation, childbirth, and menopause. Childbirth brings a woman to the threshold of physical death, and through the suffering of labor she receives the ecstatic gift of a newborn child. To a lesser degree, menstruation and menopause also follow the death and rebirth initiatic pattern. The practice of ceremonially marking life's major transitions as symbolic death and rebirth experiences and conferring on each stage of life a specific body of secret knowledge is the hallmark of all initiatic societies.

According to Aboriginal thought, every force, form, and substance, every creature and thing, is considered to have its own intelligence, its own spirit, and its own language. Whether animate or inanimate, perceivable or imperceivable, everything in the creation possesses, as do we humans, an interior invisible consciousness as well as an outer form. This way of experiencing reality is fundamental to the Aborigines and is evident throughout all the legends.

We know through the use of hallucinogens, hypnosis, and other induced trance states that a level of transpersonal perception exists widely as an aspect of human consciousness. Many methods of yoga and shamanistic rituals have revealed that the human organism possesses centers of perception through which we can become aware of an intelligence and consciousness within all forms of existence. From the point of view of Western psychology, Stanislav Grof and others have explored these altered states of being, thus broadening the modern view of the activities of the human mind. The course of our society, however, adheres to a spiritless, "rational" view of reality, leading us down a winding path of destruction. The expansive, empathetic perception of reality held by the Aborigines and other indigenous cultures appears as the most potent source to which we must now look for both humanity's and the earth's survival.

The Aborigines listened through all their senses to the various languages that permeate the natural world—for example, languages emitted by trees, celestial bodies, rocks, wind, water, fire, shadows, and seeds. In closely observing, imitating, or questioning a tangible phenomenon, one is able to listen to a message of the nature of reality as a whole.[12] The Dreamtime stories arose from listening to the innate intelligence within all things. In many Aboriginal languages the word for *listen* and the word for *understand* are the same.[13] The symbolic or poetic understanding we derive from contemplating natural form is dependent on a metaphoric model in which one thing stands for or is understood in terms of another. For example, a botanical tree, with its roots embedded in the earth and its branches reaching into the sky, may stand as the metaphysical "tree of life," the connecting link between the upper and lower worlds. We believe these metaphoric relationships are generated solely by human "intelligence" and exist only in the human language. For the Aborigines, however, the knowledge and understanding gained and reiterated as metaphor derives from an intelligible energy actually emanating from the observed form—the seed, tree, or stone—to which subtle sensory centers in our body respond.

On a day's hike into the remote wilderness of a mountainous national park I began musing on this subject. After walking for hours, I fell and lay, as if embraced, in the thick, soft layers of red and gold leaves. I opened my eyes and met with a strange sensation that rippled through my body. My mind full of language and concepts began to dissolve into a world of twisting forms, of stretching, giant cassarina trees, sensual dancing eucalyptus trees, and the entangled, bleached bodies of those trees that had fallen. I had to pull out for a moment to remind myself to listen and smell. Then it began—a nearly subliminal chattering of voices that seemed to radiate from the trees themselves. Some were transformed into ideas in my mind, others reached into my heart and groin with a sort of wordless understanding. While merging into the consciousness of this wondrous forest, I also felt distinctly human and very feminine. I felt a rush of joy for having glimpsed a world in which the Aborigines must live every day and every moment.

This feeling, however, was shared with splatterings of pain and anger at having been born into a culture that recognizes conscious intelligence in humanity only and denies its existence in all other things animate and inanimate. It is from this one-dimensional view of the world that we continue to rape, pillage, mechanize, dissect, and alienate the natural environment. Our minds are crowded with fears from our failed attempts to rationalize a world that extends far beyond reason and external appearance. Women, in particular, through childbirth and the internal experience of sexuality, have a way of knowing of the feelings that breathe within a living organism. When women are denied these feelings, alienated from the earth, and isolated in the patriarchal traditions of the competing, autonomous, self-achieving individual, the same feminine forces can become an aspect of the turmoil and destruction we see all around us.

The challenge modern femininity confronts when viewing the most ancient tradition of the Aborigines is to acknowledge that feminine wisdom, balance, strength, and intuition are dependent upon being grounded in earthly nature and a spiritually ordered society. From an involvement with these Aboriginal stories, my feelings have been reaffirmed that the primary goal of women today is to reestablish a sane and responsible relationship to the earth and to begin, if only in our dreaming, a reconstruction of an initiatic and metaphysically grounded social order.

ENDNOTES

1. Robert Tonkinson, *The Maradudjara Aborigines: Living the Dreaming* (New York: Holt, Rinehart & Winston, 1978), 35.
2. Marija Gimbutas, *The Language of the Goddess* (San Francisco: Harper & Row, 1989), xx.
3. Jennifer Isaacs, *Australian Dreaming—40,000 years of Aboriginal History* (New York: Landsdowne Press, 1987.
4. Muir, *My Bush Book*, 144.
5. Ibid.
6. The latter estimate is based on the findings of archaeologist Gurdip Singh and has been supported more recently by the discovery of charcoal remains in a core drilling into the bed of the Great Barrier reef showing a recorded increase in fire levels 150,000 years ago that can be attributed to

burning off by the Aborigines. G. Singh, N.D. Opdyke, and J.M. Bowler, *Journal of the Geological Society of Australia* (April 1981): 435-452; and *Quantum*, A.B.C. Television Series (July 1992).
7. Robert Lawlor, *Voices of the First Day: Awakening in the Aboriginal Dreamtime* (Rochester, Vt.: Inner Traditions International, 1991), 15.
8. Ibid., 266
9. Ibid.
10. Ibid., 283.
11. *Royal Commission Report into Aboriginal Deaths in Custody,* 11 volumes (Canberra: Australian Government Publishing Services, 1991).
12. Conversation with Darren McLeod, Aboriginal writer (February 1992).
13. Fred Myers, *Pintupi Country, Pintupi Self* (Washington, D.C.: Smithsonian Institution Press, 1986), 107.

ONE

TALES OF THE ANCESTRAL POWERS

Only through a mystical connectivity with the creative energies emanating from earthly places can we remember and envision the forces and powers of consciousness, the great Ancestors, who are responsible for this creation. Our ability to hold and to live in the memory of the primal creative source is an essential thread that binds together the fabric of all existence. The earth remembered as the symbolic voice of the Ancestors is our home, our place in creation. If we forget, if we lose our home, according to Aboriginal tribal elder and lawman David Mowarljarli, all of the beauty and wonder, all the stories of human and earthly life, could slip into the void of the great unconscious and be remembered by no one.

WAHWEE AND NERIDA:
THE WATER MONSTER
AND THE WATER LILY

When they were a girl and boy, Nerida and Birwain used to play beside a deep water hole. They used to dig in the muddy margin for mussels and never knew how angry they were making Wahwee, to whom the hole belonged.

There used to come often a roar of thunder, and when it was very loud, they used to drop their mussel shells and run home to their mothers' camps. But they did not know that this roaring thunder was really Wahwee's voice, threatening them with a flood if his mussel shells were not given back; for Wahwee was the greediest of water spirits; he would allow no one to touch anything belonging to him.

The old blacks knew that and had told the children never to go near his hole. But Nerida and Birwain thought only that there were to be found the biggest mussels, so they used to steal away and play there until the thunder frightened them back.

The time came when they were sorry that they had not listened to the warnings given them, but then it was too late.

A long while ago, soon after the time when fairy tales were born, the blacks knew that the world had been drowned by a big flood and only a few people saved; so when Wahwee threatened to make another big flood and drown them all, they

were afraid and avoided going near his water hole, all but
Nerida and Birwain.

Wahwee could see up through the water. He used to watch
them, and he saw that Nerida was growing into a young
woman, and he saw, too, how much Birwain cared for her.

The more Wahwee looked, the more he thought of Nerida,
and one day he made up his mind that sometime he would
steal Nerida away from Birwain.

Wahwee was so clever that he could do all sorts of wonderful things, so he began to make his plans.

All this time Nerida and Birwain grew fonder and fonder of
each other and only waited for Birwain to be made a young
man that he might ask Nerida's family for her.

Whenever they could steal away unnoticed, they went to the
haunted water hole, where they thought they were safe from
prying eyes, knowing that all the rest of the camp were frightened to risk going near it. They little knew that the greedy eyes
of the water monster were always on them.

One day, when Nerida was waiting for Birwain, an old
woman she had never seen before sat down beside her and
began to cry bitterly.

Now, Nerida was a kind-hearted girl, and she felt sorry for
that old woman; so she went toward her and offered her some
nicely cooked yams she had, saying:

"You are hungry. See, I have food. Eat."

"I have no hunger. I cry to think of the destruction you have
wrought to your tribe. And you seem so happy; and yet you
must die with them, and your loved one Birwain, too."

Nerida shrank back; she was frightened. Who was this old
woman whom she had never seen, and who yet knew she
loved Birwain, a secret she thought only he and she knew?

But her curiosity was stronger than her fear. She must find
out what the old woman meant.

"How have I harmed my tribe?"

"Did you not always steal the mussel shells from the home
of Wahwee? Did he not warn you in his voice of thunder? Yet
did you not steal, in spite of warnings from your tribe? And

now they, the innocent, and you, the guilty, must alike suffer. Cruel that you were to carelessly doom your people to destruction! And yet you offered me food; would that I could save you."

"Kind Bargie [elderly woman or grandmother], save me, and save my people. Even let me perish rather than the tribes. Save them; save Birwain and our people."

"True, there are other daughters of the tribe for him. But he stole with you; he should suffer."

"Let me suffer, me alone. Save the others, kind Bargie; save them."

"Come here tomorrow at this hour, and I will tell you if it can be done. Wahwee is raging in wrath below, declaring he will make a flood that will destroy the world again, and this time no one shall be saved; all, all will be drowned. But I will tell Wahwee how you grieve for the wrong you did and would give your life to right it."

As she finished speaking the old woman turned into an eel and slid into the water hole.

Then Nerida knew she must be a witch, such as she had heard of, so instead of waiting for Birwain, she went home, sadder than ever before in her life, fearing she knew not what, yet fearing it intensely.

The next day she went to the water hole, hoping that the day before had been a dream, but there sat the old woman.

"Kind Bargie," said Nerida, "tell me, are Birwain and my people saved?"

"It depends on you. If when I plunge into the water hole, you have the courage to plunge after me, then all may be right. Wahwee says you yourself must come and ask him this favor. If you fail to do so, he will lift his voice of thunder and call on his brothers, the rain winds, to blow up such a storm as never the world saw before, a storm after which not one living thing shall be left."

Nerida looked at the water hole, thought of the water monster, shuddered, and turned as if to go.

Then came a distant rumbling of thunder. She looked toward the camp and thought of her lover and her people, sighed, turned to the witch, and said,

"Go; I will follow."

Surely such an evil smile was never seen on a face before, but Nerida was too sad to notice its malice before the witch was gone and an eel slid into the water.

One more look at the water, one long shudder, one more look toward the camp, one long thought of her lover, one plunge, and Nerida was gone.

Later came Birwain to look for her, but all he found were her tracks coming to the water but none returning. Then he knew Nerida was gone, and he cried a death wail.

The camp people heard him and wondered, until they saw him return alone, when he told them of the tracks he had seen.

"Wahwee has seized her," they said, "Wahwee, the water monster. You will never see her again."

"My love is greater than his," said Birwain. "He drew her into the water; my love shall draw her out."

And every day Birwain sat where he had seen the tracks of Nerida, and lowly he chanted a love song:

> Here I wait for you, Nerida;
> Love of my life, I wait;
> Here will I wait till you come;
> Come, my Nerida, come.
>
> Who so supple of limb as you, Nerida?
> Who so soft of eye?
> Curly your hair was, Nerida,
> And glossy your skin.
>
> None were like you, Nerida, my Nerida;
> Love of my life, I wait;
> Heart's blood I'd spill for you, Nerida;
> Come, my Nerida, come.

Day after day Birwain sat and sang. The tribes said he was mad, mad from the loss of Nerida. They were kind to him and brought him food, but he spoke no word to them, nor they to him.

One day as he sang, watching the water, he saw it stir, and a little green leaf, like the palm of a hand, unfolded itself and spread on the water; each day came another; then came a flower bud, which, as he sang,

> *Heart's blood I'd spill for you, Nerida;*
> *Come, my Nerida, come,*

opened into a beautiful red water lily, which he thought smiled at him.

Birwain jumped up, and cried:

"It is Nerida, my blossom; she has come for me. My waiting is over; I go to her. I go!" And he plunged into the water.

But Wahwee would not have him there; he hunted him from the water hole. But Nerida clung to him on the edge, and there he was changed into a water rush; and soon that pool was a mass of red water lilies, margined with green-stalked, brown-topped rushes. And always where the water lilies are, there, too, you may see the rushes.

And if you gather water lilies, just for the old legend's sake, gather, too, a handful of water rushes, that Nerida and Birwain may never be parted.

 COMMENTARY

The fulfillment of the union that beautiful young lovers experience in an ecstatic embrace has been seen in cultures throughout the world as an approach to the ultimate state of absolute oneness. The Creative Unity, or Initial Cause, is beyond language and even beyond the gods. This mystical experience is accessible through the merger of the primal dualities: male and female, yin and yang, the sun and the moon. In spite of all their intensities and powers, the gods or Ancestors are only permanent aspects of this universal wholeness and enviously yearn for the utter bliss of completeness that opens up for romantic lovers. From Roman to Indian to Mexican to Aboriginal mythology, all the gods and Ancestors have been depicted as jealously craving the ecstatic depths of passion and rapture that romantic love inspires.

In this legend we encounter the wrath and envy of Wahwee the water monster toward the lovers Nerida and Birwain. We are taken on a familiar journey through the joys and agonies of true love, witnessing the sacrifice of the beautiful virgin Nerida to Wahwee, a dark lord of the underworld. Once again a multitude of archetypal and human characteristics and interactions that have appeared in other ancient mythologies throughout the world are pre-existent in Aboriginal Dreamtime stories. Nerida's sacrifice resembles that of the very beautiful Greek goddess Persephone, who is raped by Hades and taken to his underworld kingdom. Subsequently, after her release by Zeus, Persephone is able to alternate between one-third of the year in the underworld kingdom of darkness and two-thirds in the upper world.[1] Persephone's ascent from the underworld takes place with the annual return of springtime. Originally, she held within her single being the keys to heaven and hell, the polarities of the negative and positive sides of the Feminine.[2] The abduction of Persephone indicates that these absolute powers of the Universal Feminine must be separated in the natural world and subjected to the laws of duality, seasonal change, and alternation between dark and light. Nerida is also released from the underworld in the form of the red lily, which opens and closes with the fluctuations of night and day and the seasons.

From the inflation and rapture of their romantic love, Nerida and Birwain behaved as if they were outside or above the laws of society and nature, and this Aboriginal story depicts their death and transformation, through initiation. The initiation is led by Bargie, the dark feminine whose hidden nature is revealed by her change into a slippery eel. In Egypt and other cultures, the eel is venerated as a divine savior and redeemer of the soul. In Maori legends, the eel was also seen as one who redeems through sacrifice.[3] In our Aboriginal story, the eel performs the act of salvation by arranging the sacrifice of Nerida and thus preventing a catastrophic flood.

The Aboriginal Ancestor Wahwee has close correlations with the Greek seagod Poseidon, who also was known for his possessiveness and greed. When money was owed to Poseidon (who was also called "the earth shaker"), he sent a sea monster to plague the city of Troy and capture the Goddess Hesione.[4] In a similar manner, Wahwee threatens death and despair by way of a flood to Nerida's entire tribe, simply because the lovers secretly consumed mussels from his water hole.

The second mythic theme in our story, that of a deluge or flood, has captured the imaginations of many cultures throughout the ages. Water, the medium of life, nourishment, and growth, can swiftly convert into a deluge of death and destruction. The Biblical version of a devastating downpour of rain, with which we are most familiar, is only one of such stories that reach back to the archaic. The desolation wrought by such a flood is often seen as a cleansing and preliminary to rebirth. Indo-European cultures believed the "watery Chaos" would consume the earth at the end of one of its cycles, allowing for a new world to be reborn.[5] In Aboriginal culture, also, the flood is recognized as a device for the termination of a cycle. In this legend of the lily and the water monster, Wahwee is satiated with the sacrifice of Nerida, and the waters of destruction are withheld.

In addition to mythic elements, this legend also contains social values and strictures, such as the great importance to Aborigines of sacred sites. Removed from reality by the bliss of their love, Nerida and Birwain repeatedly defied warnings by their tribe to avoid the water hole, sacred to Wahwee. Each prominent land form such as a deep cavern, rocky outcrop, or unusually shaped hillside is considered to be a direct creation of a particular Dreamtime Being and holds spiritual significance for individuals or groups who are descendants of that Ancestral Being. This relatedness of people to land forms and regions through a metaphysical or spiritual ancestry replaces the Western concept of ownership. There is no grammatical form to express possession of anything in Aboriginal language, let alone the possession of land. The rights to, responsibilities for, and access to the land by particular groups of people is all predetermined by metaphysical stories related to each region of the countryside. Some sacred sites emanate positive energies, allowing for revelatory experiences related to fertility and initiation, while others are considered places of danger and have been outlawed. If an area deemed a sacred site is visited by either an uninitiated person or one to whom that area is taboo, there are serious consequences. K. Langloh Parker describes several water holes that were said to be haunted by beings who swallowed victims whole or sucked them down in a whirlpool. For the Aborigines these water holes are strictly forbidden as bathing places.[6]

In addition to trespassing on a sacred site, the lovers committed the theft of gobbling Wahwee's mussels. This act seems innocent; however, Aboriginal children are culturally conditioned from an early age against such behavior. Mothers employ repeated practices to impress upon their children the nonpossessive, nonacquisitive values that are characteristic of Aboriginal people. For example, Parker observed women hunting down a centipede, singeing it in a fire, and tapping their infant's hands with the stiffened body of the insect. The hundreds of creeping limbs of the centipede symbolize the instinct of grabbing or taking, while the mother's act of singeing the insect represents a law of nature that punishes the excesses of greed. As she does this, she croons:

> Gheerlayi ghilayer
> Wahl munnoomerhdayer,
> Wahl mooroonbahgoo,
> Gheerlayi ghilayer.

Which means:

> Kind be,
> Do not steal,
> Do not touch what to another belongs,
> Leave all such alone,
> Kind be.[7]

While Nerida displays disrespect by continuing to devour Wahwee's mussels, she does exhibit kindness and generosity to the old woman Bargie. "Free giving" and generosity are fostered in Aboriginal children at a very young age. The act of sharing is an instinctive reflex of Aboriginal people. Hunger does not exist among any members of a clan or tribe; everything that is hunted is shared automatically through the kinship system. This conflicts with contemporary society, which, built upon competition and self-interest, encourages individuals to accumulate the spoils of their accomplishments. Charity in our society is not the norm but is considered an extraordinary act for which people are given special recognition. Parker's observations of the mother-child relationship reveal attitudes about giving that are in sharp contrast to ours. She noted that whenever a baby for the first time picks up and extends an object, as if to give it to someone, the mother or grandmother takes what the baby offers and performs the following ritual: joyously she makes a clicking sort of noise with her tongue rolled up against the top of her mouth and croons over and over again another mantralike charm, which affects the child subliminally:

> Oonahgnai Birrahlee,
> Oonahgnoo Birrahlee,
> Oonahgnoo Birrahlee,
> Oonahmillangoo Birrahlee,
> Gunnoognoo oonah Birrahlee.

Which means:

> Give to me, Baby,
> Give to her, Baby,
> Give to him, Baby,
> Give to one, Baby,
> Give to all, Baby.[8]

Mantric incantations appear in this legend as young Birwain, in isolation, chants his love song. These are well-known ascetic devices used in both Eastern and Western spiritual practices. The trancelike state he reaches allows for contact with the spirit of his beloved Nerida, transformed into the red water lily. Traditionally, red has been associated with passion, vitality, and sexuality. The lily has, in numerous cultures, been a symbol of femininity, dedicated to the virgin goddess and representative of the female genitals. In Crete the lily was sacred to the "sweet virgin," who was chased by Minos, just as the lily is sacred to the glossy-skinned Nerida, who is desired and pursued by Wahwee. The water lily of Africa was the sacred lotus of ancient Egypt, representing fertility and resurrection because of its connection with the life-giving river Nile. In Biblical times the lily symbolized power against evil, and its sacred associations led to its employment in protective witchcraft.[9] In many cultures the lily was also called the passion flower and associated with intense passions and love, such as those expressed in this story.[10] In fact, all of these associations are consistent with the symbolic function of the lily in our Aboriginal story.

Nerida and Birwain in their eternal forms of the water lily and the phallic, brown-topped rushes represent the theme of all romantic philosophies: that the union of the feminine and masculine in love persists into death. The Aborigines are reminded of this metaphysical truth as they gather the delicate lilies from among the rushes, relishing them as much for their sensual texture as for their nourishment.

ENDNOTES

1. Max S. Shapiro and Rhoda A. Hendricks, *A Dictionary of Mythologies* (London: Paladin Books, 1981), 154.
2. Barbara Walker, *The Woman's Encyclopedia of Myths and Secrets* (San Francisco: Harper & Row, 1983), 786.
3. G. A. Gaskell, *Dictionary of All Scriptures and Myths* (New York: Avenel Books, 1981), 241.
4. Shapiro & Hendricks, 160.
5. Walker, *The Woman's Encyclopedia*, 316.
6. K. Langloh Parker, *The Euahlayi Tribe: A Study of Aboriginal Life in Australia* (London: Constable, 1905), 137.
7. Ibid., 54.
8. Ibid., 52.
9. Rex Warner, *Encyclopedia of World Mythology* (London: Peerage Books, 1975), 240.
10. Walker, *The Woman's Encyclopedia*, 542.

DINEWAN THE MAN CHANGES TO DINEWAN THE EMU

One tribe once stole up to another tribe at night and, surprising them, slaughtered many. Afterwards a singer of the slaughtered tribe made a song in which he sang of the dead of his enemies, the mention of whom was considered a cruel insult.

A singer of the insulted tribe then arose. He too had made a song. In his song he sang of all the dead of the other tribe.

Then when the anger of both tribes was rekindled by these insults, a big fight took place in which all those whose dead had been mentioned fought. One man did not join in the fight, for none of his dead had been mentioned, but in the general confusion someone's spear struck him on the chest and he fell dead. His mother rushed to him, calling, "Who killed my son? Who killed my son?"

But no one knew. Her tribe came round her, but she waved her arms and said, "Go, all of you. Leave my son to me."

Still they pressed around her. She turned in fury on them and by the force of her rage drove them from her. They fled and left her with her dead. Leaning over her son, she saw that his spirit had left his body. Knowing his Minggah (spirit tree), she went to search for it there. For three days she watched that Minggah, for three days she walked ceaselessly round it, and on the third day she found the spirit of her son. She took it and put it back into the body from which she had already extracted the spear, the head of which had left a deep cut at the top of her son's chest.

When the spirit was back in the man, he arose and followed his mother to rejoin their tribe. As her relations saw the mother coming toward them, they raised their voices in the death song. She silenced them, saying, "Why do you wail? My son lives."

Not so," they said; "we left him dead. Did you not bury him?"

"No, he is alive. He is there. Go you," she said to a young girl relative, "and see your relation. He is sitting down over there."

The girl ran in the direction indicated, and soon the tribe heard a joyful cry of recognition from her. One after another of them followed her and saw what she had seen—the relative they had left dead sitting alive before them.

They cried aloud: "Duggaandee gurroonahdee gnai," which meant "Glad to see you, Uncle."

But to their joyful greetings he made no answer. And as they came nearer, he rose to his feet and turned to run away. Even as he turned, they saw the man bend and saw his body change, transforming into the largest bird they had ever seen, the bird now known on the plains as Dinewan, which had been the man's name, and which bird has a dent at the top of its chest even as the spear would make in the chest of the man, Dinewan.

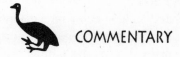 COMMENTARY

In this legend of Dinewan, the Ancestors committed what, for humans, was considered a serious infraction of the Dreaming law—that of speaking or singing the name of those deceased. The Aborigines go to extreme lengths to ensure that a deceased person's name is not spoken. For example, if someone's name is Possum, not only is it forbidden to speak this name, but the animal's name is changed throughout the entire tribe, as well. Among the Euahlayi tribe of which Parker speaks, the belief is that a deceased person's spirit emerges from the grave to meet his or her dead relations, who will then help the deceased on the difficult journey to the Realm of the Dead—or sky camp. However, if the deceased's name is called by the living, he or she may be tempted to stay as a despairing, disembodied spirit on earth, thus creating havoc among the living. It could be inferred from our myth that the death of the innocent young man, Dinewan, was an indirect, tragic consequence for breaking the taboo of speaking the name of the dead.

The various actions or roles the mother plays in this myth are indicative of women's roles in Aboriginal culture. In general, women are the guardians of the natural laws and the protectors of bodily life, while the men are the guardians of the spiritual realms, such as those of the Unborn and the Dead. During times of conflict, women are often the arbitrators, and a ritual fight may not take place unless women are present. The mother in this myth takes control of the situation, and in her impassioned fury she retrieves the spirit of her innocent son. She waits and walks around the Minggah tree for three days, which represents the completion of the initial disengagement of spirit energy following the death of the body. This duration appears in many other myths—for example, the three days of entombment after which Christ rose from the grave. We see even closer connections to the Dinewan myth in the Egyptian myth of Osiris, the god of death and resurrection, which preceded the Christian version. Osiris was raised from the dead and restored to life, not by his father but by his divine mother, Isis.[1] As in the case of Dinewan's mother, Isis's first care "was to make Osiris stand up," evoking the idea of the restoration of the erect or "true" male phallic spirit. Among the Aborigines, male spirituality and religion encourage entering into, through initiation, the deep behavioral patterns that generate, protect, and nourish all embodied life and are referred to as the mother law. The maintenance of this law is the first concern of both Dinewan's mother and the mother of Osiris. They represent the creative aspect of the feminine that becomes detached from the idea of possessing their progeny and instead transmutes personal attachment to a more universal level of nurturance for society and nature. This is in contrast to our myth of "The Wirreenun Mother and her Wirreenun Son" (page 96), in which we see the Aboriginal exploration of the dark feminine power acting through the principle of motherhood.

In this legend of Dinewan, the boy died of what the Aborigines consider unnatural causes, that is, a disruption of the Dreamtime law. In addition to effecting a balance on the metaphysical dimension, the mother's goal in restoring her son's spirit was to ensure that archetypal order penetrated to the emotional and humane levels: to "raise up" the boy so that he might bid farewell to his relations and to ease the shock of his spirit undergoing such an untimely and unnecessary death. The retrieving of a spirit and returning it to one considered dead is often witnessed in Aboriginal life. In *More Australian Legendary Tales,* Parker gives an account of a baby who was brought back to life. The baby had "breath put back into it" by two wirreenuns (medicine persons). Parker interviewed a few witnesses, who all corroborated the story, describing how "the wirreenuns had caught the breath just after it left the baby and put it back through the child's mouth. They then set to work to suck the sickness out of the body, allowing the baby to recover."[2]

An interesting characteristic of the emu bird is the manner in which it feeds. When an emu bird that is feeding has eggs to hatch, it will, with all its young chicks, trek back and forth to the nest, ensuring that the eggs are safe. This quality of returning to the nest is portrayed in central Arnhem Land (in northern Australia) by the funerary dance that imitates the emu and symbolizes the psychic tendency of the spirit to repeatedly return to the body after death.[3] For this reason, the Aborigines bury their dead in two stages. The preliminary interment allows for a period of coming and going of the spirit prior to the final reburial, when the spirit completely recedes to the Realm of the Dead. In a variety of ways, the emu represents an intermediary stage between the spiritual and physical worlds, especially in that it is a flightless bird. For the emu belongs, in part, to the bird family, which is airborn and spiritlike, while at the same time it is wingless and physically grounded.

When a young boy kills his first emu he is told to lie on top of its warm body. In doing so, he deeply empathizes with the death of his prey.

Subsequently, the young hunter's raising himself up from the dead bird represents rebirth, in that his life will be continually nourished by this death. A method of cooking the emu also demonstrates its symbolic connection to rebirth. When an emu has been hunted and killed, the Aborigines carefully pluck the feathers and slit the skin from anus to throat. They pull the skin off in one piece, like a sweater; it is then turned right side out and stuffed with grass and feathers, and the opening is reclosed with pegs. In this ritual preparation, the emu, at death, assumes another bodily form. This is an excellent example of the rigor with which the Aborigines acknowledge spiritual and mythic content in their daily life.

Birds, in general, represent an image of rebirth, in that they are considered to be born twice, first as an egg and then as a chick. The innocent young man, Dinewan, is turned into an emu through his mother's demand that the Dreamtime law be respected. The characteristic indentation at the top of the breast of the emu (symbolizing the young man's pierced chest) represents the heart-rending outcome of an infraction of the Dreamtime law. His rebirth in the form of one of the great ancestral archetypes (the flightless emu bird) offers consolation to the living, in that the emu will be seen on the plains eternally, and his spirit will be evoked each time its beautiful feathers are used as decoration in ceremonies or its large green eggs are devoured as a delicacy.

ENDNOTES

1. Barbara Walker, *The Woman's Encyclopedia of Myths and Secrets,* (San Francisco: Harper & Row, 1983), 750.
2. K. Langloh Parker, *More Australian Legendary Tales,* (London: David Nutt, 1898), xii.
3. Judith Ryan, *Spirit in Land: Bark Paintings from Arnhem Land,* (Victoria, Australia: National Gallery of Victoria, 1990), 111.

STURT'S DESERT PEA, THE BLOOD FLOWER

Great was the talking in the camp one morning of the river tribe, for during the night Wimbakabolo had fled, taking with him Purleemil, the promised bride of Tirtla. The elders sat together and planned how to capture them. While they were talking, the young men came and told them that the tracks of the fugitives were leading toward the large Boulka, or lake, where was camped a hunting expedition, part of a tribe from the back country, of whom the father of Wimbakabolo had been one.

Then the elders knew the fugitives must be going to take refuge with this tribe. They called the fighting men together, and they said, "Gather your weapons; we shall go to this tribe and demand that they give us the fugitives. Wimbakabolo shall we slay, Purleemil shall be Tirtla's to slay or keep as it pleases him."

Soon they went forward, after having painted themselves in full war paint and armed themselves with many weapons. For two days they followed the track. On the third day they saw the camp fires; then they sent their messengers to the tribe, whose elders received them and listened to their request that Wimbakabolo and Purleemil should be given up.

"Do not send me back to old Tirtla." cried Purleemil. "Two

wives has he slain with his waddy [wooden club]; let me not be the third." And she sobbed aloud.

"Cease your crying," said Wimbakabolo. "I give you up to no man; rather would I slay you with my spear. Let Tirtla," he said, turning to the elders, "be a man and fight me. I am ready, but he is a coward. Men of my father's tribe who have given us shelter, who when we were hungry gave us food, remember that in the days that are past my father was one of you, a great warrior who slew your enemies as if they were ants, so powerful was he. Even as he fought for you, so will his son in the days to come, if you give him your aid now. Long have I loved Purleemil, she with the starry eyes, and her heart has been mine ever. Can a maid at the bidding of the graybeards turn her heart to a wife-slayer, leaving the one she loves, turning from one who is young, strong, and straight to a bowed cripple? Remember my father, before you despise the help of his son before you, and his grandsons to come. We shall never go back to the tribe of Tirtla; rather will I spear Purleemil, my heart's beloved, as she stands before you, and mingle my blood with hers."

Wimbakabolo drew himself up and looked so powerful and fierce a warrior as he stood, weapons in hand, before the elders that they said, "Fools should we be to give up the son of our old leader to our enemies. He shall lead us as did his father before him, and his Purleemil shall be the mother of warriors to follow him, for strong are the clan of Wimbakabolo, men like mountains, as their name tells."

Then an elder turned to the messengers saying: "Let Tirtla come alone out on the plain; there Wimbakabolo will meet him, and there they can fight. If Tirtla will not, then let him go back, a coward, to his country and stay there. Wimbakabolo remains with us; we shall give him up to none."

Back to their tribe went the messengers, but no Tirtla came to accept the challenge, and back to the big river went he with the others.

Wimbakabolo and Purleemil lived in peace, loved of all the

tribe they had come to, for he was a mighty hunter and she a singer of sweet songs.

After a while, when the cold winds began to blow round the Boulka, the tribe moved their camp to where, on the far side, were more trees for shelter and firewood, for the winter was at hand.

Before the winter had gone, a son was born to Wimbakabolo and Purleemil, and seeing what a big baby he was, the tribe laughingly called him "The Little Chief," and brought him offerings of toy boomerangs, throwing sticks, and such things until the eyes of his mother shone with pride, and the father already began to make him weapons to be used one day against the enemies of the tribe who had sheltered them.

And Purleemil would sing her songs, and her baby would crow and laugh, and the father would say little as he carved weapons with an opossum's tooth but bear so proud a look on his face as he glanced from time to time at his wife and child, that all would smile to see his happy pride—and their hearts were glad that the elders had not given up Purleemil to be the bride of Tirtla, the wife-slayer.

The winter passed away, and with the coming of the summer all made ready to return to their hunting ground, where the fugitives had first come to them.

But Purleemil sang no longer. The spirits, she said, told her that misfortune was at hand.

"Let us stay in the winter camp," she said to her husband, "where we have been so happy. I fear we shall lose our Little Chief if we go. Let us stay, my husband."

"That cannot be, my wife, or the tribe would call me a coward and say I feared to meet Tirtla."

"Better be called a coward, which all know you are not, my husband, than lose our Little Chief. Dark would our lives be without him; he is the sun that brightens our days, without him dark as a grave would they be forever."

"That is true, my wife; now he has been with us so long, life would be dreary without him, our Little Chief. But why should

we lose him? Did not the spirits say he should live forever on
the plains? Then why should you fear for him, my loved one?"

"I cannot tell. Truly the spirits said so, and yet they say now
as their voices come to me on every breeze, that misfortune is
at hand."

"But not for the Little Chief, Purleemil. For the tribe, maybe,
who sheltered us, then how could we leave them to face it
alone? Come with me bravely, mother of the Little Chief, lest
our son drink in fear at your breast."

So Purleemil hugged her child to her and spoke no more of
her fear. And as the days passed merrily in the new camp that
was the old, the fears were forgotten, and the spirits ceased
their warnings.

One night when the tribe were all asleep, unwitting of
danger, their enemies, who had been waiting their chance,
closed around them. Closer and closer they came, led by the
crafty Tirtla; too great a coward to risk an open fight, he stole
like a dingo into the camp at night, meaning to slay by treach-
ery all who had balked him of his prey, Purleemil. She should
be slain with the rest—men, women, and children—all were to
be sacrificed to his hate. He had laid his plans well, waiting
until all fear of vengeance was over and all vigilance relaxed.

Closer and closer they crept, making no sound as they came
nearer and nearer.

The Little Chief stirred in his sleep; Purleemil crooned him to
rest again with the spirit's song, telling how he should live on
the plains forever, the brightest, most beautiful thing on them;
soon was he soothed and the mother, nestling closer to the
ever-loved Wimbakabolo, slept again unwitting of danger.

A dog at their feet growled, and Wimbakabolo stirred; again
the dog growled, Wimbakabolo rose to his feet, but even as he
stood up he was felled to the ground by a deadly blow from
Tirtla, and into the camp rushed the enemy, slaying the sleep-
ers as they lay for the most part, though some had time to seize
their weapons, in vain, to defend themselves.

Tirtla, who for days had known the camp of Purleemil and

claimed as his own victim her husband, having killed him, now with fiendish yell transfixed the body of the Little Chief with a jagged spear.

The tongue of Purleemil, the sweet singer, clove to her mouth as she saw her husband dead beside her and her child on the spear of her enemy. Then she wrenched the spear from Tirtla, and the end, which had passed through the body of her baby, she turned and plunged into her own heart, pinning the Little Chief to her, and she fell with him dead onto the body of her husband, and the life blood of the three mingled into one stream.

Thus was accomplished the vengeance of Tirtla, which left not one alive of the tribe who had given the fugitives shelter. Leaving the bodies to the hawks and crows, Tirtla and his tribe went back to the Callawatta.

The next season they determined to hunt on the hunting grounds of their dead enemies. But when they reached them, they camped some distance away from the scene of the slaughter, lest the spirits of the dead should molest them.

At night they saw strange lights moving on that spot; then they knew that the spirits were indeed abroad.

The next morning they went for water to the Boulka. How it glistened in the sun! But was it water? They paused and looked. No water was that before them. On they went and then saw that the large lake had been turned to salt. Then the tribe were frightened and turned back to their own hunting grounds, for no man likes to dare the spirits. Tirtla said he would follow them, but first would he go to where the bones of his enemies bleached; it would give him joy, he said, to see them. With hatred still strong in his heart, he went. But surely, he thought, must his eyes be dazzled with the glare from the salt lake before him, for he saw no bones in the place where his enemies had been, only masses of brilliant red flowers spreading all over the scene of the massacre, flowers such as he had never seen before.

As he was gazing with a dazed expression at them, there

stretched down from the sky a spear with a barb that caught
him in the side and lifted him from his feet. As he hung in
midair, he heard a voice, though he saw nothing, say: "Cow-
ardly murderer of children and women, how dare you set foot
on the spot made sacred forever by the blood that you spilt, the
blood of Little Chief, his mother and his father, which flowed in
one stream and blossomed as you see it now, for no man can
kill blood, for more than the life of the flesh is in blood. Their
blood shall live forever, making beautiful with its blazing
brightness the bare plains where are the salt lakes, the dried
tears of the spirits whose songs Purleemil sang so sweetly, the
salt tears that they shed when you and such as you poured out
the life blood of their loved tribe. Here shall you sit forever
before your handiwork, the work of a coward."

So saying, the spirit transfixed Tirtla to the ground, leaving
the spear still through him.

There, in the course of ages, man and spear turned to stone
as an everlasting monument of the spirit's power, and there at
Tirtla's feet spread the beautiful red flower, the glory of the
Western plains where the salt lakes are—Sturt's Desert Pea, we
call it, but to the old tribes it was known as the Flower of Blood.

 COMMENTARY

This beautiful, despairing myth of love and revenge culminates in what for
the Aborigines is considered the greatest of all tragedies—the loss of
innocent lives, the annihilation of an entire tribe, and particularly the
barbaric murder of children. How can we understand the symbolism
behind these atrocities in the light of Aboriginal cosmology?

The Dreamtime and the natural world are two distinct domains, in
which fundamental laws function in entirely different ways.[1] Similarly, in
our cosmology, the forces, energies, and magnitudes in the intergalactic

world of stars and universes function differently than those that regulate and describe the terrestrial sphere. The Aboriginal law takes into account that the archetypal world can not directly impose itself on the physical realm. While reflecting the activities of the Dreamtime creation in their way of life, the Aborigines understand the necessity to modify, through their customs and laws, the intense and extreme aspects of these mythic ancestral patterns, so that they can be incorporated and harmonized into a physical and social reality.

This view, which holds the Dreamtime reality distinct yet interrelated, is exemplified by the portrayal in the Dreamtime story of the great warrior-chief and his noble son (Wimbakabolo). In Aboriginal life, however, a hierarchy of male power such as this does not exist. There are no headmen, chiefs, leaders, or warriors. No single man is elevated to a pinnacle from which he controls and directs other people, spiritually, morally, or physi-cally. Every man stands as a self-sufficient hunter accountable to tribal initiatic growth and inner knowledge of the Dreaming laws. In Aboriginal life, infraction against Dreamtime laws may cause hostilities between tribes, but one tribe attacking or subduing another does not occur. Only during ritual can men put on the garb of the mighty warrior and enact the hero's victory of power and self-aggrandizement.

Another contrast in behavior between the Ancestors in the Dreaming and the Aborigines in life is found in marriage. In this myth, Tirtla has complete domination over his wives and his promised bride, Purleemil, much as in early Christian marriage and in the Islamic fundamentalism of today. This male supremacy is not found in traditional Aboriginal life, where elopement is permissible within kinship codes. In the living world, Purleemil would have every right to desert the wife-slaying Tirtla, in spite of her betrothal to him. In practice, any unhappy or abusive marriage can be dissolved, but not so in the extremes and excesses of the Dreamtime.

Within this archaic Dreamtime story, we can immediately recognize the son-hero myth, the son perpetuating his father's reputation and quest for immortality by slaying the forces of darkness (Tirtla). The Greek myth of Apollo the sun god, and the Christian adoration of Jesus, following in the footsteps of this father-God, are the two versions of this son-hero myth, which has been the fundamental dynamic of patriarchal society from its beginning to the present day.

> The Sun God continuously reasserts his authority over the pow-
> ers of darkness and the son, in the name of his God/father,
> armed with shield, goes forth to perform that essential Patriar-
> chal deed which identifies him with the creator himself.[2]

In our society, in government, religion, and the hero syndrome of
popular entertainment, this myth is perpetuated. The myth of the heroic
young male overthrowing the enemy is always based on the split or
polarity between the light and dark forces, good and evil, with the characteristic of darkness conventionally attributed to the feminine. As with
Purleemil, the feminine has, through the ages, been seen as needing to be
brought under the orbit of the light-bringing masculine power.

We have also become conditioned to the happy ending. The hero,
through virtue and reason, overcomes the mysterious forces of darkness
and evil, thus fulfilling our need for security, justice, and order under the
umbrella of our paternal family, government, or church. Yet in the Aboriginal myth of Sturt's Desert Pea, there is a surprising twist. The courage and
virtue of the hero lead to catastrophe. By imposing his paternal image and
hero ethic over the deep, intuitional, spirit-informed warning of Purleemil,
Wimbakabolo is actually responsible for the murder of his wife, his child,
and his protective tribe.

With puffed chest, Wimbakabolo overrides Purleemil, convincing her
that all will be well if she follows his reasonable and courageous decision.
His denial that Purleemil has genuine contact with the spirit world is
mirrored in the theme of the solar myth by the belief "the feminine must be
rescued from her own darkness." In this action, Wimbakabolo also denies
his own inner feminine, with disastrous outcome.

Wimbakabolo's heroic pronouncement of his father's power, his own
strength, and his love for Purleemil express the same values that cloud the
visions of modern society, with touching self-sacrificing illusions. Whether
it be the so-called developed nations that send people off to war for the
democratic ideal, or those countries governed by despots itching for
unadulterated power, the outcome is always one of horrific destruction,
with the leaders seducing the young men into the role of hero and savior.

As we observe contemporary society being driven to constant war and
perilous conditions by the son-hero myth, we can only marvel that a
simple Dreamtime story, perhaps a hundred thousand years ago, not only

foreshadowed this archetypal pattern but foresaw the dire consequences of its excesses.

Feminine intelligence, which is derived from the mysterious inner depths and openness to the spirit messages of nature, is charmingly portrayed by Purleemil. As is the case with women in our society, Purleemil's intuitive feelings are blocked, not only by the male dominant values but also by the feminine nature itself. If Purleemil had firmly trusted her intuitive contact with the spirits and had had the determination to convince her husband that misfortune was at hand, Little Chief and her beloved tribe might not have been gruesomely slain. Traditional Aboriginal culture demonstrates through the importance placed on dreams and the psychic and spiritual world that it values the feminine intuitive mode of knowledge and decision making beyond the external, rational, male reasoning and morals.

Each detail in this story has meaning and resonates with symbology found in myths from many ages and cultures. Once the Little Chief is transfixed by the jagged spear, Purleemil's tongue cleaves to the top of her mouth. *Lingus,* the Latin word for tongue, is derived from the Sanskrit *lingam* (phallus) and is also the root of the word for language and logos. Placing the tongue (phallus) between the lips (labia) represents coitus and is a sacred gesture symbolizing both the procreative act and the act of creating spoken language.[3] Purleemil's beautiful language of song unites the unseen spiritual world with the visible material world. Her tongue, cleaving in horror at the deaths of her husband and son, represents her song turned back upon itself.

The symbolic act of Purleemil wrenching the spear from Tirtla and, with her baby on the end, plunging it into her own heart can also be related to other cultures. In Egypt, for example, the heart was considered to be "the source of all life and thought," and particular care was taken in its mummifying. The Egyptian image of a woman carrying her child "under her heart" arose from their belief that menstrual blood came from the maternal heart and was therefore the source of the child's life.[4] Furthermore, the Egyptians believed that because the heart pumps the life essence, or blood, in opposing directions, its flow of energy gives birth to mind and intelligence. When the blood, or life essence, springing from the emotional center of the heart, unites with the mental principle, intuition arises.[5] This entire mosaic of blood, heart, and intelligence symbols is evoked when Purleemil stabs herself through the center of her intuition, which had been denied by her husband.

In the Dreamtime, the characteristics and qualities that the Ancestors displayed were extreme, distinct, and absolute, in contrast to the physical world, which is a blending of these archetypal and primal qualities and patterns of behavior. Purleemil's act of great courage, strength, and control is symbolic of the feminine power when a cycle approaches its end. By plunging the spear deep within her, she draws the extreme archetypal characteristics of her loved ones and her adversary back into herself: the pure innocence of the Little Chief, the absolute courage and vanity of Wimbakabolo, and the unmitigated evil of Tirtla. Thus, she conjoins and balances these Dreamtime forces in preparation for the emergence of a new creation. The tragically spilled blood is transformed into a bloom of brilliant red flowers—both historically and mythologically a symbol of death and rebirth. The sleep-inducing quality of opium from the red poppy, for example, represents death, while its silken flower is believed to spring from the blood of slaughtered warriors and gods and has been used as a symbol of remembrance of those killed in the battle of Flanders during the First World War.[6] In this Aboriginal legend, the red Sturt's Desert Pea alludes to the death or conclusion of the Dreamtime in order that the natural world may come into being.

The salt lakes in this legend extend and reinforce the theme of rebirth. It has been known for millennia that salt preserves living tissue, and Egyptian mummies were preserved in a brine solution called "birth fluid." Salt water was accepted as a substitute for the mother's regenerative blood; it came from the womb of the sea and had the taste of blood. Superstitious fear of spilling salt was directly related to the idea of spilling blood.[7] Therefore, salt became a symbolic instrument of universal kinship, in that we are all related through the sacrifice of maternal or menstrual blood.

The very ancient icon of the mother pelican piercing her own breast so that her drops of blood will feed her nest of newborn chicks was usurped by Christianity and replaced by the sacrificial or bleeding heart of Christ.[8] The single phrase from this archaic Aboriginal story, "for no man can kill blood, for more than the life of the flesh is in blood," foreshadows the long, mysterious history of the symbols that attempt to convey the hidden and spiritual energy related to blood and blood sacrifice. In Aboriginal reality: "On the physical level it is blood that communicates between the Dreaming and the perceivable world. Just as the body 'drinks' the nourishing energy of the blood to maintain itself, so too the blood 'drinks' subtle energies from the spirit world in order to maintain the nourishing communication between them."[9]

ENDNOTES

1. Robert Lawlor, *Voices of the First Day: Awakening in the Aboriginal Dreamtime* (Rochester, Vt.: Inner Traditions International, 1991), 45–46.
2. Marion Woodman, *The Ravaged Bridegroom: Masculinity in Women* (Toronto: Inner City Books, 1990), 19.
3. Barbara Walker, *The Woman's Encyclopedia of Myths and Secrets* (San Francisco: Harper & Row, 1983), 1002.
4. Ibid., 375
5. G. A. Gaskell, *Dictionary of All Scriptures and Myth* (New York: Avenel Books, 1981), 344.
6. Rex Warner, *Encyclopedia of World Mythology* (London: Peerage Books, 1975), 247.
7. Walker, *The Woman's Encyclopedia*, 886.
8. *The Encyclopedia Britannica: A Dictionary of Arts, Science, Literature & General Information,* Eleventh Edition, Volume 21 (Cambridge, England: University Press, 1911), 68.
9. Lawlor, *Voices of the First Day,* 334.

WHERE THE FROST
COMES FROM

The Meamei, or Pleiades, once lived on this earth. They were seven sisters remarkable for their beauty. They had long hair to their waist, and their bodies sparkled with icicles. Their father and mother lived among the rocks away on some distant mountain, staying there always, never wandering about as their daughters did. When the sisters used to go hunting, they never joined any other tribes, though many tried from time to time to make friends with them. One large family of boys in particular thought them so beautiful that they wished them to stay with them and be their wives. These boys, the Berai-Berai, used to follow the Meamei about and, watching where they camped, used to leave offerings there for them.

The Berai-Berai had great skill in finding the nests of bees. First they would catch a bee and stick some white down or a white feather with some gum on its back between its hind legs. Then they would let it go and follow it to its nest. The honey they found they would put in wirrees (bark containers) and leave at the camp of the Meamei, who ate the honey but listened not to the wooing.

But one day old Wurrunnah (fiery Ancestor) stole two of the girls, capturing them by stratagem. He tried to warm the icicles off them but succeeded only in putting out his fire.

After a term of forced captivity, the two stolen girls were translated to the sky. There they found their five sisters stationed. With them they have since remained, not shining quite so brightly as the other five, having been dulled by the warmth of Wurrunnah's fires.

When the Berai-Berai found that the Meamei had left this earth forever, they were inconsolable. Maidens of their own tribe were offered to them, but as they could not have the Meamei, they would have none. Refusing to be comforted, they would not eat and so pined away and died. The spirits were sorry for them and pleased with their constancy, so they gave them, too, a place in the sky, and there they are still. Orion's sword and belt we call them, but to the Daens (Aborigines) they are still known as the Berai-Berai, the boys.

The Daens say the Berai-Berai still hunt the bees by day and at night dance corroborrees, which the Meamei sing for them. For though the Meamei stay in their own camp at some distance from the Berai-Berai, they are not too far away for their songs to be heard. The Daens say, too, that the Meamei will shine forever as an example to all women on earth.

At one time of the year, in remembrance that they once lived on earth, the Meamei break off some ice from themselves and throw it down. When, on waking in the morning, the Daens see frost everywhere, they say: "The Meamei have not forgotten us. They have thrown some of their ice down. We will show we remember them, too."

Then they take a piece of ice and hold it to the septum of the noses of children who have not already had theirs pierced. When the septums are numb with the cold, they are pierced, and a straw or bone is placed through them. "Now," say the Daens, "these children will be able to sing as the Meamei sing."

A relation of the Meamei was looking down at the earth when the two sisters were being translated to the sky. When he saw how the old man from whom they had escaped ran about blustering and ordering them down again, he was so amused at

Wurrunnah's discomfiture, and glad at their escape, that he burst out laughing and has been laughing ever since, being still known as Daendee Ghindamaylannah, the laughing star (Venus) to the Daens.

When thunder is heard in the winter time, the Daens say: "There are the Meamei bathing again. That is the noise they make as they jump, doubled up, into the water, when playing Bubahlarmay, for whoever makes the loudest flop wins the game, which is a favorite one with the earth people, too." When the noise of the Bubahlarmay of the Meamei is heard, the Daens say, too, "Soon rain will fall, the Meamei will splash the water down. It will reach us in three days."

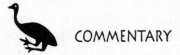

COMMENTARY

Authors Giorgio de Santillana and Hertha von Dechend, in their groundbreaking book *Hamlet's Mill,* have brilliantly documented that in all societies and epochs, movement and patterns of the heavenly bodies have provided a fundamental source for myths and the formation of culture.[1] The depths of the celestial oceans represented the inconceivable aspect of the universe. Perhaps for humanity to render spiritually bearable the ineffable dimensions of existence, ancient cultures wove threads of their familiar inner and outer experience through the infinite spaciousness of the heavens. The legend of the Pleiades places the Aborigines within this worldwide tradition, the difference being that the antiquity of Aboriginal lore reaches into depths of time far beyond other cultures, where astronomically based myths were recorded 2,000 to 8,000 years ago. These cultures include those of Babylonia, Syria, China, Polynesia, neolithic Europe, ancient India, Egypt, and Greece.

More surprisingly, this myth has many specific components that strongly resemble those found in astronomical myths from these cultures. How do we explain the mythological similarities between Aboriginal lore and other diverse and distant cultures? One possibility is Carl Jung's idea of a pool of resonant thought forms passing through the generations, which he named the "collective unconscious." Aboriginal culture explains correspondences such as this through its concept of "songlines," magnetic and vital force flows that emanate from the earth, crisscrossing the continent. Aborigines believe that they can project their psyche or inner consciousness along these songlines as a means of communicating songs, stories, and knowledge over great distances. It is said that songlines were once a sacred tradition that stretched across the entire earth, and, in this way, cultural knowledge was shared worldwide.

An example of cross-cultural symbolism found within this legend stems from pre-Vedic India, where the Pleiades were called the Seven Mothers of the World. They were seen as "priestesses who judged men, sometimes critically wounding them," with their blazing rays, referred to as "castrating moon sickles."[2] This image corresponds closely with that of the ice-covered Pleiades in the Aboriginal myth, who in their cold aloofness and rejection of the Berai-Berai boys psychologically castrated them. As a result, the Berai-Berai denied themselves other women and died pining for the seven sisters. In Indian mythology the fire god Agni tried to warm the Seven Mothers by copulating with them.[3] This is similar to the fiery Aboriginal Ancestor Wurrunnah, who, in our legend, tried to melt the ice off the Pleiades with fire. The Egyptian texts also allude to the Pleiades' archaic significance as "judges of men, assigning them to the seven planetary spheres as the seven Hathors." After death, those wishing to enter the paradisiacal garden of heaven were to name the seven sisters before entrance was granted. In Borneo, the seven sisters were also associated with the abode of the dead.[4]

In Greek mythology, the Pleiades were placed in the heavens by Zeus when Orion, the hunter, fell in love with and pursued them, much as the Berai-Berai (also hunters) pursued the sisters in the Aboriginal legend.[5] Furthermore, the Berai-Berai were "translated to the sky as Orion's belt and sword." The Greeks also named one of the sisters Merope, which means "bee-eater." Honey, collected by the Berai-Berai in our legend and left as a gift to the Pleiades, is, in many cultures, a symbol of spiritual or celestial nourishment; bees were emblems of purity and messengers of the Gods.[6]

Another important ancient Greek myth, that of the virgin goddess Artemis, connects with the Aboriginal Pleiades. Artemis was the protectress of powerless or pregnant women and youth (particularly young girls), as well as of all nature. She was named the Huntress of the Seven Stars and personified the independent feminine spirit, free from men and male domination. The Aboriginal Meamei were also aloof and cold, disdaining lovers, maintaining at all times a strong sisterhood. In Greek mythology, it is claimed that Orion, lover of the Pleiades and also Artemis, was accidentally shot in the head by one of Artemis's arrows, just as the Meamei were accidentally responsible for the death of their pursuing lovers.[7] The Aboriginal culture acknowledged in practice many of the attributes of Artemis. For example, women spent time in isolation, particularly while menstruating. Women also spent much time in the company of other women. In addition, it was women who were responsible for mitigating the violence of tribal conflicts to ensure that justice took place. In the same way that Artemis embodied certain qualities of the female psyche, the "Meamei shone as an example for all women."

An important image in this story is the utilization of the icicles of the Meamei to pierce the nose or septum. This significant Aboriginal initiatic process was performed to improve resonance in singing, that is, to enable those initiated to "sing as beautifully as the Meamei." In Mesopotamia, the Pleiades were also associated with resonance or vibration in music. The most sacred drums were made with the hide of a black bull with seven circles inscribed on the drum face. The bullhide represented the zodiacal configuration of Taurus the bull, of which the Pleiades are the central body of stars. It is said that the striking of this drum set up a vibrational contact with the Pleiades, the "most significant part of the heavens."[8] These correspondences extend into Indian mythology, ancient Egypt, and the cosmology of the North African Dogons. The Aboriginal culture maintains that the spirits of the dead journey along straight energy paths that pass through the Pleiades on their way to the constellations of Canis Major and Canis Minor. Within these constellations is the great star Sirius, which in all these cultures is designated as the "gateway" to the Realm of the Dead.[9]

K. Langloh Parker points out that nose piercing and the placing of bone through the septum affects not only sound resonance but also the sense of smell. Smell is the most precise and minute power of human sensitivity and is actually a response to the molecular vibration of a substance. Smell is so subtle that it is related by the Aborigines to spiritual or psychic energy. When the Aborigines visit a strange camp, they place bones through their noses so they will not smell the strangers and thereby partake unconsciously in a psychic energy exchange. Interestingly, Parker points out that the Aborigines claimed "the smell of white people made them sick." She further comments, "And we, in our arrogance, thought it was the other way around."[10]

The practice of bone wearing was so important to tribal Aboriginal women that they adamantly defended it long after European contact. Parker gives an account of an old Aboriginal woman who had a pierced nose and was abruptly questioned by a white laundress as to why she wore a bone and not earrings like white people. "The black woman looked the laundress up and down and finally anchored her eyes on the earrings. "Why you make hole in your ears? No good that. Black gin no do that, pull 'em ears down like dogs. Plenty good bone in your nose make you sing good. Sposin some one smell bad, you put bone in nose no smell them. Plenty good to make nose longer, no good to make hole in ears, make them hang down long like dogs." And off she went, laughing and, pulling down the lobes of her ears, began to imitate the barking of a dog."[11]

People of many cultures have been moved by the patterns of the celestial bodies. In other myths we will explore not only the similarities between the Aboriginal culture and others but also the differences that result from their incredible antiquity. Only in Australia is there a pre-neolithic culture that was alive, intact, and undisturbed until two hundred years ago. Their mode of perception, in which all of the world is alive with spirit, is imprinted in their language and culture. We, as a society, have amputated this level of experience from our consciousness, resulting in a world that aches with the life-threatening problems of pollution, desecration, and overpopulation. However, when we look into the night sky glittering with celestial bodies, we can experience the timeless sense in which the great dreaming of human culture has unfolded and will continue to unfold. With this vision, our fearful and hungry imaginations fill with a mythic dimension, and the seeds of change are born anew.

ENDNOTES

1. Giorgio de Santillana and Hertha von Dechend, *Hamlet's Mill* (Boston: Gambit, 1969), 46–50.
2. Barbara Walker, *The Woman's Encyclopedia of Myths and Secrets* (San Francisco: Harper & Row, 1983), 803.
3. Ibid.

4. Ibid.
5. Max S. Shapiro and Rhoda A. Hendricks, *A Dictionary of Mythologies* (London: Paladin Books, 1981), 158.
6. G. A. Gaskell, *A Dictionary of All Scriptures and Myths* (New York: Avenel Books, 1981), 368.
7. Shapiro and Hendricks, 145.
8. Giorgio de Santanilla and Hertha von Dechend, 124–125.
9. Joseph Campbell, "Mythologies of the Primitive Hunters and Gatherers," *The Historical Atlas of World Mythology,* Vol. 1, *The Way of the Animal Powers,* 33.
10. K. Langloh Parker, *The Euahlayi Tribe: A Study of Aboriginal Life in Australia* (London: Constable, 1905), 37.
11. Ibid, 36.

TWO

TALES OF THE ANIMAL POWERS

By means of an oral tradition, the Aborigines passed from generation to generation the genealogy of human bloodlines as they flowed from particular animal species or totems. These Dreamtime legends are a collective memory, which link humans and animals to the same common origin—the metaphysical Dreamtime Ancestors. Presently, we have reduced our commonality with animals to the theory of our superiority through evolution. In contrast, the Aborigine's relationship to animals and nature is one of communion, kinship, and a sense of belonging. Though our society has obliterated this memory, the animals, even today, remember, and they wait patiently for the shadows of rationality and brutality cast across our minds and spirits to dissolve.

MURGAH MUGGUI,
THE SPIDER

Murgah Muggui was a bunna, or cannibal, and lived by herself in a pine tree scrub.

She was a great wirreenun, or witch. This was the way she gained the victims she desired for food.

When she saw a young man going hunting through bush, she would change herself from an ugly old witch into a beautiful young woman. Then she would go toward the young man and ask him where he was going.

"Hunting," he would say, upon hearing which, she would propose to accompany him, and off they would go together. When they came back, she would suggest, "It is late; you had better camp with me tonight."

"No," he would say, "I have a wife. I must get back to her with some food."

"Well, just wait while I cook a little bit for you to eat before you go."

The man, feeling hungry, would agree to this. Having eaten, he would feel disinclined to move, especially when the beautiful young woman begged him to stay, telling him he could easily say to his wife that he had camped in the bush, and she would never know he had not camped alone. He might stay one night with her when she was lonely, she said. She had her way—he stayed. When he was soundly asleep, Murgah Muggui stole away from her fireside, picked up her gunnai, or yamstick, which was very sharply pointed at the end, and stole back with it to the sleeping man.

He opened his eyes and saw before him an old woman with her gunnai poised to strike him.

His surprise was so great at seeing a hideous old hag that he lay paralyzed as the gunnai came down, pinning him dead to the earth.

So gained Murgah Muggui many victims, on whose remains she feasted.

One day Mullyan, the strong and clever man of the tribe, came that way. He saw a beautiful young woman who advanced toward him. She asked him what she had asked the others, went hunting with him, and persuaded him, as she had them, to camp the night there.

But Mullyan was suspicious of her—he only feigned sleep. He watched the beautiful young woman steal away; he saw her pick up her gunnai, and, as she did so, turn into a hideous old witch, who, with a leer of triumph, came stealthily toward him.

Down came the gunnai, but ere it touched his body, he had seized it. He jumped up, pulled the gunnai from the grasp of the astonished old hag, turned its point upon her, and drove it through her heart, killing her on the spot where so many had fallen victim to her.

Her spirit was turned into Murgah Muggui, the spider, who lives on the pine ridges, where she spins her fine web traps from tree to tree, devouring, as of old, her many victims caught within the gold and silver meshes she makes so cunningly.

 COMMENTARY

The experience of Aboriginal culture is comparable to entering into a crystalline lattice, where every detail of life—its creatures, plants, and earthly locations—is embellished with mythic connectivity and multiple. dimensions. Just as the spider manufactures a variety of silken threads, each one specific for a given task, so too the Aboriginal Dreamtime stories contain a multitude of levels of understanding and qualities of knowledge for the task of living consciously. In this commentary on Murgah Muggui, we explore prominent features on four levels of understanding—biological, social, psychological, and spiritual.

Most species of spider capture and devour their prey in three distinct phases. Aboriginal knowledge of these characteristics is evident in the correlations between the spider's habits and the manner in which the female Ancestor Murgah Muggui lures, captures, and then kills her prey. First, the spider spins her beautiful and graceful web, coating some of the threads with a sticky substance, and waits, "listening" for her approaching victim. By placing herself in an inconspicuous position, the spider is able to feel, with her legs, any vibrations that might occur throughout the entire web indicating she has ensnared a victim. In our myth, Murgah Muggui spins a fantasy of feminine entrancement by presenting herself with an aura of beauty and gracefulness. Her web provides the intended victim with companionship on his lonely hunt and invites him to the comforts of her campsite.

In nature, the spider's second step is to throw herself upon her quarry, rendering it helpless by wrapping it tightly in a mass of fine silk threads. So, too, Murgah Muggui tightens the woven mesh around her victim by satiating his appetite and inducing deep sleep. Third, the spider bites her captive with her sharp jaws, just as Murgah Muggui stabs her victim with her sharpened gunnai.

Spiders feed cannibalistically on other insects by injecting peptic juices into their prey and sucking the juices up later when all the nutrients of the prey's body are dissolved. The indigestible exterior skeletons are then thrown out of the web.[1] Consequently, the spider must often renew and rebuild her web, then wait again in anticipation of her next victim. Murgah Muggui, like a spider, repeatedly employs the same tactics of laying her deadly web of feminine illusions. These are a few examples of how, metaphorically, the structure and details of this story accurately reflect the observed behavior of many species of spider.

On a social level, the Aborigines define their behavioral codes in response to the dramatic and sagacious events of the Dreamtime. In traditional Aboriginal society, men are permitted to have a number of wives simultaneously, but once married, they are prohibited from extra-marital affairs. Murgah Muggui in this myth is successful in tempting her unwitting victim to discard his marital responsibilities, leading to his unfortunate end. Another social code played upon in this legend concerns the sharply pointed gunnai that Murgah Muggui uses to stab her victim. Whereas restrictions are placed on male aggressive behavior, Aboriginal women are allowed to freely vent strong emotions, but they are strictly prohibited from using or carrying spears, axes, flint knives, or fighting weapons. The essential tools utilized by women are dilly bags, wooden bowls, and digging sticks. A digging stick may, if necessary, be used against other women, but it is considered primarily a domestic tool and is indicative of women's ritual monopoly in food gathering. Thus, the structure of this legend examines a succession of behavioral strictures held by the society and displays the dire consequences when these codes were originally enacted by the Ancestors.

The instinctual pattern of mating for a male spider can often be a deadly affair, as female spiders of many species have the reputation for devouring the male during sexual intercourse.[2] This behavior has some interesting inferences in human psychology. Through the ages, the vagina dentata, or "toothed vagina," has in many cultures represented the archetypal, often unconscious male fear that during intercourse a woman may devour or castrate her partner.[3] The Aborigines express this same image as the vagina inferno, and historian H. R. Hays quotes an Aborigine as saying, "The vagina is very hot, it is fire and each time the penis goes in, it dies."[4] These symbols are derived from an overriding association between death and the feminine found in many cultures. The dark cavity of the vagina leads to that mystifying core of a woman from which she is able to transform a seed into a living being. However, the origins of death arise with the life-giving power hidden within these inner parts: for all that is born of woman dies. It is the fear of death that men divulge in their trepidation of the female genitals, and myths such as those relating the spider to the devouring female appear in cultures where the association between death and the feminine is consciously or unconsciously active.

In Aboriginal spirituality, each level or cycle of initiation requires the male to confront the four primary aspects of the Universal Feminine—virgin/prostitute, wife, mother, crone. The spider with her eight legs represents the infinite possibilities of feminine or earthly power for change: the four directions and four seasons. So, too, the four aspects of the feminine represent the passage of life from birth to death—childhood, adolescence, maturity, old age. Murgah Muggui displays all four of the feminine roles: spying her victim through the bush, she appears as an ever-youthful, beautiful virgin or sacred prostitute, symbolic also of the wilderness in which they both hunt. Next she suggests it is late and he should stay the night, as would the dutiful, caring wife. When this is refuted, she gives food and comfort, as would a mother. Finally, as the old hag, she represents the forfeiting of all of life to the process of decay and inevitable death.

On a spiritual level, Murgah Muggui in this myth performs the role of an initiator. She represents the passage through which the male must view the inevitability of death (the crone), which is hidden in all that is alluring, enchanting, earthy, and beautiful. In the ancient Indian tradition, the "fanged and bloody Death Goddess is the same as the beautiful mother and lover."[5] To be able to superimpose and adore both images in one is considered the strongest beginning on the road of spiritual enlightenment. Murgah Muggui spins the destiny (Latin *destino,* meaning that which is woven) of those men who are searching for initiation into the secrets of the dark feminine. In the old fairy tale of the spider and the fly, the fly was said to be symbolic of the soul "which was in search of a female entity to eat it and give it rebirth."[6]

Mullyan, the strong and clever man in the Aboriginal myth, remains conscious or awake, his senses alert, symbolizing the male, initiatically prepared to confront death and thereby be reborn into a new awareness. Unlike his predecessors, Mullyan does not allow sleep to obscure his realization that the beautiful virgin transforming into the old hag are one and the same. Instead, he confronts and accepts the hag's presence, her power, and her necessity. Symbolically, in slaying the crone, Mullyan has overcome his fears of the dark feminine as she eternally reclaims the life that she has given to all.

Once again portrayed in this simple Aboriginal Dreamtime story is the essential image of initiatic death and rebirth. Throughout history, in all religions, these ritual practices have been deemed necessary to unlock a crucial transformative dimension of the human psyche. The initiatic theme was perpetuated in Christianity by the story of Christ's death and resurrection and treated as either a historical event for the populace or a universal symbol for the more educated. However, in the pre-Christian archaic world, of which Aboriginal culture is the oldest example, near-death experiences or deep hallucinogenic trances were invoked, allowing the initiate an actual, personal confrontation with death. In initiatic culture, the awareness of the ubiquitous presence of death was the element that brought living to its fullest intensity. In ancient Rome, Taoist China, and other cultures, men were disciplined to repeat to themselves, "Man, remember you will die."

What has been so often ignored is the role of women or the Universal Feminine in the initiation of men into the deep mysteries of death. The word *hag* or *crone* in a contemporary dictionary indicates an ugly old woman or witch. However, in ancient cultures such as the Egyptian, Hag was respected as a "holy woman," the mother of wisdom, law, and words of power. The Goddess Hecate in Greece was the queen of the dead and was embodied in the human form of wise women or high priestesses. "The Great Goddess was intimately involved in every manifestation of death as she was in life. . . . Women cradle the infant and the corpse, each to its particular new life."[7] In northern Europe, hags were considered priestesses of sacrifice, and the face of Hag, the death goddess, was veiled "to imply that no man can know the manner of his death."[8] This resonates with Murgah Muggui, who spins her web of deception disguised as a beautiful young woman, her captive male oblivious to her true form.

In many mythologies, Fate is represented by the triple goddesses, who were weavers. The archaic worship of Aphrodite saw her as three Moirae or Fates—the Spinner, the Measurer, and the Cutter of life's threads. In Hindu myth, Maya was represented by the spider. She was the spinner of magic, fate, and earthly appearances. In other cultures the spider was seen as the goddess who sat at the center of her web, or wheel of fate. Among the Malekula people of the South Seas, the spider is seen as a negative feminine power who was identified as the mother of death and through initiations as the bringer of the boon of rebirth.[9]

A spider always builds her web on an inclined angle similar to the inclination of the earth's axis that creates the endless phenomena of the seasons of life. Through the gold and silver mesh of a spider's web, we can envision—in her weaving, entrapping, and killing—the constant alternation of the cycles of life both for creatures and for the cosmos. We may view the spider's parlor of silvery threads as either a sticky, discomforting, and even deadly trap or as an emblem of the many concentric planes of being, woven within a continuous existence. Whichever way we perceive it, as a prison or a sparkling jewel, the spider's web is a "language" that allows us to see the expansiveness of the eternal plan in one gossamered moment.

ENDNOTES

1. Karl Von Frisch, *Animal Architecture* (New York: Harcourt Brace Jovanovich, 1974), 28–33
2. *Encyclopedia Britannica,* 11th ed., vol. 25 (Cambridge: Cambridge University Press, 1911), 665.
3. Barbara Walker, *The Woman's Encyclopedia of Myths and Secrets* (San Francisco: Harper & Row, 1983), 1034.
4. Rex Warner, *Encyclopedia of World Mythology* (London: Peerage Books, 1975), 30.
5. Walker, *The Woman's Encyclopedia,* 217.
6. Ibid., 958.
7. Ibid., 215.
8. Ibid., 366.
9. Buffie Johnson, *Lady of the Beasts* (San Francisco: Harper & Row, 1988), 214.

BRALGAH,
THE DANCING BIRD

Bralgah Numbardee was very fond of going out hunting with her young daughter Bralgah. Her tribe used to tell her she was foolish to do so—that some day the Wurrawilberoo would catch them.

It was not for old Bralgah Numbardee that the Daens cared, but all the camp were proud of young Bralgah. She was the merriest girl and the best dancer of all her tribe, whose women were for the most part content to click the boomerangs, beat their rolled-up opossum-skin rugs, and sing the corroborree songs in voices from shrill to sweet, while the men danced; but not so Bralgah. She must dance, too, and not only the dances she saw the rest dance, but new ones that she taught herself, for every song she heard she set to steps. Sometimes, with laughing eyes, she would whirl round like a boolee, or whirlwind. Then suddenly she would change to a stately measure. Then for variety's sake she would perform a series of swift gyrations, as if, indeed, a whirlwind devil had her in his grip.

The fame of her dancing spread abroad, and proud indeed was the tribe to whom she belonged; hence their anxiety for her safety, and their dread that the Wurrawilberoo would catch her.

The Wurrawilberoo were two cannibals who lived in the scrub alone.

But in spite of all warnings, Bralgah Numbardee continued to hunt as usual with her only daughter for companion.

One day they went out to camp for two or three days. Nothing hurt them the first night, but the next day the Wurrawilberoo surprised and captured them. They gave Bralgah Numbardee a severe blow. She fell down and feigned death, lest they should strike her again and kill her. The Wurrawilberoo picked her up to carry her off to their camp. They did not wish to hurt young Bralgah; they meant to keep her to dance for them. They told her so, and gave her their muggil, or stone knife, to carry, telling her to fear nothing and come with them.

She went with them, but when they were not looking, she threw the knife away.

As soon as they reached the camp, the Wurrawilberoo asked her for it. They wanted to cut up Bralgah Numbardee before cooking her. Bralgah said she had put the muggil down where they had rested, some way back, and had forgotten it.

They said, "We will go back and get it. You stay here".

They started. When they were some way off, the mother said, "Are they out of sight yet?"

"Not yet. Wait a little while."

Bralgah watched them go away, then told her mother, who immediately jumped up. Off then went both mother and daughter as fast as they could to their own tribe, whom they told what had happened.

When the Wurrawilberoo came back, they were enraged to find not only the daughter but the mother gone, even she whom they had left, as they thought, dead. No feast, no dance for them that night unless they recovered their victims, from whose tracks they found that Bralgah had actually been able to run beside her daughter.

"She only feigned death," they said, "to deceive us. We will hasten and overtake them before they reach the tribe. Yea, even if they are with the tribe we will snatch them away."

But the Daens were looking out for them, fully armed, seeing which the Wurrawilberoo turned and fled, the Daens after them in quick pursuit, but they failed to overtake them; and, fearing to follow them too far lest a trap lay ready for them, they returned to the camp. But so wroth were they at the attempt to capture their prized Bralgah that a council was held and the destruction of the Wurrawilberoo determined. Two of the cleverest wirreenuns said they would send their Mullee Mullees in whirlwinds after the enemy to catch them.

This they did. Whirling along went the boolees with the Mullee Mullees in them. Quickly they went along the track of the Wurrawilberoo, whom they soon headed, turning them back toward the camp whence they fled.

"We will go," said one of the Wurrawilberoo to the other, "back to the camp, ahead of these whirlwinds. We will seize the girl and her mother, and fly in another direction. The whirlwinds will miss us in the camp and seize others. We will not be balked. Young Bralgah shall be ours to dance before us, and her mother shall make our supper tonight."

On, on they fled before the whirlwinds, which gained both size and pace as they followed them.

The Daens were so astonished at seeing the Wurrawilberoo returning straight toward them, the whirlwinds after them, that they never thought of arming themselves. Into the midst of them rushed the Wurrawilberoo. One seized Bralgah the mother, the other young Bralgah, and before the astonished Daens realized their coming, they had gone some distance along the edge of the plain.

"Bring your weapons," roared the Mullee Mullees in the whirlwinds to the Daens as they swirled through the camp after the enemy.

The Wurrawilberoo carrying young Bralgah were ahead. One finding the whirlwinds were gaining on them, dropped his burden, Bralgah Numbardee, and ran on. Just in front of them were two huge balah trees. Feeling that the whirlwinds,

which they now knew must have spirits in them, were already
lifting them from their feet, the Wurrawilberoo clung to the
balah trees, the one who had captured young Bralgah still
holding her with one arm while he grasped the tree with the
other.

"Let the girl go," shouted the other to him. "Save yourself."

"They shall never have her," he answered savagely. "If I
have to lose her, they shall not get her."

Then as the whirlwinds howled round them, tearing up
everything in a wild fury, the balah trees now in their grasp
creaking and groaning, Wurrawilberoo muttered a sort of
incantation and released young Bralgah. As she slipped from
his grasp, came a shout of joy from the Daens, who were just
in the wake of the whirlwinds; they had their spears poised but
had been frightened to throw for fear of injuring Bralgah.

But their joy was short lived. The whirlwinds wound round
the balah trees to which the Wurrawilberoo clung, and dragged
them from their roots before the men could leave go. Up, up
the whirlwinds carried the trees, the men still clinging to them,
until they reached the sky; there they planted them not far from
the Milky Way. And there they are still, two dark spots, called
Wurrawilberoo, for the two cannibals have lived in them ever
since, being dreaded by all who have to pass along the
Warrambool, or Milky Way. There are camped many old Daens,
cooking the grubs they have gathered for food, and the smoke
of their fires shows the course of the Warrambool. But one can
only reach these fires if the Wurrawilberoo are away, as sometimes happens when they go down to the earth and, through
the medium of boolees, pursue their old enemies, the Daens.

When the Daens saw that their enemies were gone, they
turned to get Bralgah; her mother was already with them.

But where was young Bralgah? She had not been seen to
move away, yet she was gone. All round the plain they looked.
They saw only a tall bird walking across it. They went to the
place whence the trees had been wrenched. They scanned
the ground for tracks but saw none of Bralgah going away—

only those of the big cranelike bird now on the plain.
Wurrawilberoo must have seized her again and taken her
after all, they said.

As soon as the Mullee Mullees, which had animated the
whirlwinds, returned from placing the balah trees and the
Wurrawilberoo in the sky, the Daens asked them if they had
left her there.

No, they said, Bralgah had not gone to the sky. Surely the
Daens had seen Wurrawilberoo let her go.

Then where was she?

That no one could say, and no one thought of asking the big
bird on the plain. All mourned for Bralgah as for one dead. Her
spirit, they said, would haunt the camp, because they could not
find her body to bury it, though they knew she must be dead,
otherwise would she not return to them?

They moved their camp away to the other side of the plain.

After a while they noticed a number of birds like the one
they had seen on the plain at the time of Bralgah's disappear-
ance, and, after feeding for a while, these birds would begin to
corroboree—such a strange corroboree, of which one bird
taller than the others was seemingly a leader.

This corroboree was so human and like no movements of
any other birds, like indeed nothing of the sort that the Daens
had ever seen, unless it were the dances of the lost Bralgah.

Out onto a clear space the leader would lead her troupe.
There would be much craning of necks and bowing, pirouet-
ting, stately measured changing of places, then gyrating with
wings extended, just as Bralgah had been wont to fling her
arms, before she madly whirled around and around as these
birds did now, seeing which likeness, the Daens called,
"Bralgah! Bralgah!"

The bird seemed to understand them, for it looked toward
them, then led its troupe into wilder and more intricate figures
of the corroboree.

As time went on, the leader of the birds was seen no more,
but so well had her troupe learned the corroborees that they

went through the same grotesque performances as in her time.

When Bralgah Numbardee died, she was taken to the sky, there to live forever with her daughter Bralgah, both known to us as the Clouds of Magellan and to the Daens as the Bralgah.

There Bralgah Numbardee learned that the Wurrawilberoo by his incantation had changed her daughter into the dancing bird, which shape she had to keep as long as she lived on earth.

Afterwards, if ever the Daens saw a boolee speeding along near their camp, the women would cry, "Wurrawilberoo," clutch their children, and bury their heads in their rugs; the men would seize their weapons and hurl them at the ever-feared and hated capturers of Bralgah.

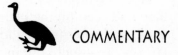 COMMENTARY

When reading this myth, one is immediately drawn to the suffering that the whirling Bralgah incurs because of her outstanding talents and her propensity to always capture the limelight in public performances. In our competitive society, this type of behavior is encouraged and given highest rewards. From an Aboriginal perspective, however, Bralgah's tragic fate and her drive to excel are interdependent. When viewed in this way, Bralgah's story allows us a fresh means of questioning and contemplating a social phenomenon that is central to our sense of individual development, that of fame.

Etymologically, *fame* was originally defined as the ability to "speak over a vast distance," while modern dictionaries associate it with "renowned reputation" or "excellence." In contrast to these positive connotations, we encounter in this legend the grave consequences of Bralgah's notoriety, which was a fundamental attractor of the dangerous desires of the Wurrawilberoo. Young Bralgah gyrates and dances with wondrous skill and discipline. Her dances are so gracious that she retains the love and respect of her tribe in spite of a deep need that drives her to break accepted codes and perform both male and female dances, sometimes even altering traditional steps and movements and devising new ones.

It is not that Aboriginal tribal life disallows men and women the opportunity to experience self-glorifying roles or a magnified sense of one's individuality. These experiences are relegated to or occur during initiations or ritual performances. During the ceremonies of his or her rites of passage, each person is the unquestioned center of attention of the entire tribe. In many of the other rituals, the roles of the dominant performers shift, so that each person has opportunities for beauty or excellence and recognition. Access to the type of self-esteem derived through recognition by others is, therefore, a birthright of all.

The Aborigines believe that the exaggeration of self-importance, which we call fame, distorts the flow of interrelationships and shatters the sense of belonging that forms the web of the society. A fixation on the role of hero or heroine can block an individual from fulfilling other life roles. This is made evident in our legend, in that Bralgah at a mature age is still hunting alone with her mother. This most certainly symbolizes that Bralgah has forfeited her other life roles as wife, mother, and lover to her obsession to dance and perform publicly. The unhealthiness of their relationship is reinforced by the seemingly incestuous fashion in which Bralgah's mother feeds on the association with her daughter's fame and fortune, disallowing the company of anyone else on their hunting excursions.

In Western society the multitude of contenders for the crown of fame is dwarfed only by the even greater mass of people interested in worshipping those who succeed. In this way fame becomes the structural dynamic not only of entertainment but also of religion, politics, and business. In such a society people are deluded into deriving a sense of their self-esteem from the heroes or heroines who answer their dreams or live out their hopes and desires. Fame, therefore, results in the "stealing of power" by the few from the many; we have lost the sense of balance concerning the role of the godlike or elevated performer. This archetypal role, symbolized by the famous dancing Bralgah, has become so inflated that all other aspects of our life fall under its power.

The second interesting aspect of performance raised within this story involves the phenomenon of spirit possession. Throughout history many great theatrical performers have described the experience of performance as one of being in the possession of spirits. Similarly, a shaman, in order to heal or reveal sacred knowledge, must be possessed by powerful spirits. Both the performer and the shaman reach into the netherworld, dissolving their individual identity and opening themselves to habitation by other forces in order to form a bridge of communication between the unseen realms and physical life. These correlations are not surprising, since the roots of theatrical performance arose from shamanic ritual.

Very often, as in the case of Bralgah, the performers as well as the shamans may become trapped by the mask they wear. They may lose sight of the fact that the amplification of their powers is through possession, believing the power and the mask to be theirs.[1] In this myth Bralgah insisted at all times on dancing; she was not content to sing with the women or take a supporting role. Her mask began to control her, as indicated in the story by the words "as if, indeed, a whirlwind devil had her in his grip." This problem is acknowledged in various indigenous cultures; for example, the Native Americans also took measures to prevent the inflation that can result when a tribal member is given the opportunity, in ritual performance, to represent a godlike totem ancestor. Following such a ritual, the performer would, for days, weeks, or perhaps months, be obliged to assume the most menial task, such as grinding corn, in a subdued, self-effacing manner. The next season the totem or clan would allow another member of the tribe the privilege and power of performance.

K. Langloh Parker's research verifies the Aborigines' deep cultural involvement with the phenomenon of spirit possession, which I will summarize here, as it corroborates this interpretation of the Bralgah story. Each person has at least three spirits: the Yowee, or the equivalent of the soul; the Doowee, a dream spirit; and a Mulloowil, or shadow spirit. Some may also have an animal spirit, or yunbeai. A wirreenun, or witch doctor, gains initiatic knowledge, so that they have complete control over their own dream spirit, or Doowee, which is then called a Mullee Mullee.[2] In our myth the Mullee Mullees were placed by two of the cleverest wirreenuns into whirlwinds, which they instructed to chase the treacherous Wurrawilberoo. In contrast to the more initiated wirreenums, a less initiated person's dream spirit or Doowee may wander at will, creating the devastating or peaceful adventures we all encounter in our dreams. Sometimes, however, it may be captured or attacked by the directed Mullee Mullee of a wirreenun. If in the morning one awakes tired and languid, it is claimed that the Doowee has been on the rampage or under attack by another. The only way in which people may guard against the capture by or rapscallion undertakings of their Doowee is to sleep with their mouths tightly shut—that is, provided they do not meet the Mullee Mullee of a wirreenun greater than their own.[3] A thorough and complex knowledge of the interactions between dream spirits is essential for Aborigines in understanding the events, conflicts, and good fortunes of their daily lives.

Women, in particular, are afraid of whirlwinds inhabited by spirits (called boolees), as they could cause them to give birth to twins, an event they consider both undesirable from the point of view of their wandering lifestyle and unfair to the second-born child.[4] The boolees are often considered messengers of the coming of death as well as the vehicle that can capture and carry away a person's spirit at death. Parker describes the death of an old woman and how the Aborigines perceived the role of a boolee, or spirit-inhabited whirlwind in that death:

> Round it whirled, snatching the dead leaves of the Cooloobahs, swirling them with the dust it gathered into a spiral column, which sped, as if indeed a spirit animated it, straight to the camp of the dying woman. Round and round it eddied, a dust devil dancing a dance of death. . . .
>
> All was silent but the swirling leaves as the column gathered them. Finding the deathbed guarded, the boolee turned sharply from the camp and sped away down the road, dissolving on the poliogonum flat in the distance. . . . The old woman was dead.

Our story concludes with Bralgah transformed into the Australian crane, or Native Companion, which bears her name. Before departing to her place in the celestial Dreamtime, Bralgah taught her exquisite dancing to a group of cranes, or bralgah. These birds today perform their intricate and gyrating group dances without the presence of a leading performer. The source of their spectacular choreography and group harmony is invisible. Likewise, Aboriginal society functions harmoniously without a hierarchy of leaders and heroes, because, through Dreamtime stories and ritual, they are in tune with the invisible, spiritual forces of nature. Once again our story begins with the observation of a marvelous and mysterious character-istic of an animal species and leads us through the equally mysterious passages of our own collective and personal psyche and nature.

ENDNOTES

1. Walter F. Otto, *Dionysus—Myth and Cult* (Dallas, Texas: Spring Publica-tions, 1981), 84.
2. K. Langloh Parker, *The Euahlayi Tribe: A Study of Aboriginal Life in Australia* (London: Constable, 1905), 35.
3. Ibid., 27–28.
4. Ibid., 52.
5. Ibid., 84.

PIGGIEBILLAH,
THE PORCUPINE

A man and a woman went hunting one day. After having secured as much food as they wanted, they started back to the camp. On their way, they came to a big dead Noongah tree. They saw oozing out of the bark signs of bargullean, a kind of edible grub.

The man said he would chop some out. He took his willahderh (big tomahawk) and began chopping. His wife, who was quite a young girl, sat down near him.

"Get farther away," he said, "I might hit you."

He went on chopping, but soon stopped again to warn her. "Get farther away."

"I am all right," and she went on eating grubs as they dropped beside her. The man gave an extra hard chop and out of his hand flew the willahderh, striking his wife and nearly severing her breasts.

He thought she would die. He said he must hasten to the camp and bring back her mother and father. But first he would carry her down to the creek, where he would make a shade for her to lie under.

Having done this, he hurried away. After he had gone, she noticed that numbers of bargullean were crawling over her wounds. She managed to get up and drag herself to the creek,

where she washed them off and at the same time cooled her
wounds, then crawled back exhausted to her shelter.

Piggiebillah, an old woman, came along. She saw floating on
the creek some of her favorite grubs.

"How did my bargullean get here?" she wondered.

She gathered some up, then she went to the Noongah tree.

"Who has been chopping my Noongah tree?"

She looked around, went back to the creek, and followed it
up until she reached the wounded woman's shelter. Seeing her,
she said, "Myjerh! What is the matter?"

"My husband has nearly killed me. He did not mean to. He
has gone to fetch my father and mother to see me before I die."

"You will not die. I will make you well."

Piggiebillah came closer to her and held the wounded
breasts in their places while singing a healing incantation over
them. Then she said, "You will be all right."

And the girl at once felt better; the pain was gone; she soon
felt as if the accident had never happened; she was quite well.
But at the same time a great dread of Piggiebillah possessed
her, for she knew the old woman must be a great wirreenun
witch.

"Stay here," said Piggiebillah to her, "while I go for my
comebee [bag]; then I will return and take care of you."

But as soon as Piggiebillah was out of sight, the girl, feeling
quite strong again, dragged a log into the shelter her husband
had made, laid it where she had lain, covered it with her
opossum rug, and fled in haste to her tribe.

Reaching them safely, she told of how she had been cured,
but that she was frightened of the old woman who had cured
her and fled before she returned.

Her tribe told her that she had reason for her fear, for surely
had she remained there she would have been killed. The old
woman was Piggiebillah, a great wirreenun who punished with
death anyone who dared to touch her Noongah tree or the
bargulleans from it.

They told the girl that even now she was not safe from the

witch's vengeance. But they told her what to do, giving her two small pointed bones. They said, "Lie on your back, hold a bone in each hand, and when Piggiebillah hunts you out, as surely she will, blind her by sticking a bone in each of her eyes."

Piggiebillah, having armed herself with her witch yamstick, went back to where she had left the girl, whom she indeed meant to kill. She saw the log and thought it was the girl asleep under the rug. She tried to drive her witch stick into it, but to her surprise she felt something hard; she hit at it again, still the hard resistance; she lifted the rug, and there was only a log!

She knew then she had been tricked. Grasping her witch stick savagely, off she started on the girl's tracks.

She reached the camp; through it she strode silently, up to where the girl lay. She poised her deadly stick, ready to drive into her victim.

But ere she had time to strike, the girl sprang up and stabbed her in both eyes, rendering her powerless for the moment to do anything. And before she could recover, the tribe raised their spears and aimed them at Piggiebillah, who, as the weapons touched her, fell dwarfed to the ground, where her form changed from that of a woman to that of a porcupine, a small animal covered with spearlike spines, with driven-in eyes. In this form the old witch quickly sped from the camp and was soon out of sight. Ever since, the porcupines have been known by her name of Piggiebillah.

 COMMENTARY

The key to interpreting this legend of Piggiebillah is the Aboriginal understanding that death and initiation are one and the same thing. In Aboriginal tribal life young women are guided through the initiatory experiences of menstruation and childbirth under the auspices of an older female, such as an aunt or grandmother, who assumes the archetypal role of Piggiebillah, the hermit wise woman. In some menstruation rituals, similar to the events in our story, the young woman's betrothed husband will construct a hermitage hut in which the older female relative will take the young girl through her initiation into womanhood.

This ritual is extended over several months, during which time the young woman is covered with mud, smoked with special leaves, and able to eat only the food brought to her by her older female initiator. No sweets such as honey are allowed for four moons. After some time, the women of the tribe make her a camp closer to the big one, whereupon she is dot-painted with red ochre and white gypsum and adorned with sprays of sweet-smelling white flowers on her arms and head. White swansdown is scattered over her head, and a sprig of a sacred tree is placed through the hole in the septum of her nose. The old woman gives her a bouquet of smoking leaves to carry as she walks toward the main camp. As she walks, the other women sing her songs in a strange language. The young woman then encounters her betrothed husband sitting on a log with his back to her. As the singing builds in momentum and pitch, the young girl hurls her bouquet to the ground, grabs her betrothed husband on his shoulders, and shakes him. She then runs away. In a few weeks time, she is shifted again to a camp closer to the main camp. A fire is made for her, on the other side of which is camped her betrothed husband. This gradual bringing together of the couple increases the dramatic intensity and mystery surrounding their inevitable union. They camp like this for one moon, at the conclusion of which the old woman informs the young girl that she must camp on the same side as her husband and become his obedient wife. In return he must also treat her well, or her relatives will take her from him.[1]

In a sense the loss of the young woman's breasts could be interpreted as a reversion to a younger, pre-initiatic state. This event, perhaps, indicates that her prior formal initiation did not bring about the necessary inner changes, and critical life circumstances were required to complete her maturation. The young wife's appetite for the grubs that fall from Piggiebillah's tree is insatiable. Her hunger may be interpreted on a psychological level as her desire to be drawn into a confrontation with the dark and solitary sorcerer in order to return to the ceremony she had not inwardly inscribed.

The isolated female hermit with extraordinary occult, psychic, or healing powers is a character often met in Aboriginal Dreamtime stories and
one that is antithetical to the sociocentric thrust of Aboriginal awareness.
As mentioned previously, the Aborigines' primary identity is that of their
clan, tribe, or kin group, in contrast to contemporary society, which is
centered on the autonomous individual.

The Aboriginal commitment to collective awareness does not mean that
the archetypal forms of isolation and hermitage are repressed or banished;
rather, they are relegated to spiritual or ritual forms of expression. Social
codes modify these pure prototypal energies and blend them into human
behavior. For example, for a period of time after the death of her husband,
a woman takes a vow of silence, which often has a healing effect in grief
or during a severe transition. Women have been known to undertake this
vow for twenty to twenty-five years.[2] At the same time, the demands of
group relatedness are maintained through a complex sign language ac-
quired by all tribal Aborigines in addition to their spoken languages.

Another symbol in this legend that reinforces the theme of the isolated
female sorcerer is the accidental severing of the young wife's breasts by the
erring tomahawk. In Greek mythology, Artemis, the solitary huntress of the
wilderness, represents a similar archetype of feminine consciousness.
Artemis was often portrayed, as were the Amazon deities from the Black
Sea region of southeastern Europe, with her right breast removed in order
to gain the full drawback on her bow and arrow. Such a removal was
administered to all women who chose the path of the isolated huntress.[3]
This ritual slashing of the breast signifies independence from the confine-
ments of social order and freedom from bondage to the archetypal, nourishing mother. Artemis also represents the focusing of female energy on her
individual and spiritual development and the achievement of occult powers. While Artemis is aloof and disdainful of society, her detachment
allows for her role as the guide, protectress, and initiatress of girls and
women as they pass through the trials of the nurturing, feminine phases in
life.

It is interesting to explore the transformation undergone by the archetype of the female hermit since its origins in the Aboriginal Dreamtime.
Many of the attributes and functions of Artemis, the hermit, belonged in
earlier times to Diana of Ephesus, who was depicted not with severed but

with multitudinous breasts that "nourished" all of life.[4] Historically, as the feminine powers were subjected to constant conflict and assault by patriarchal society, this image of Diana was transformed into that of Artemis (with breast removed), who retreated to a position of alienation from and antagonism to the social process.

It is to this archetype, the self-sufficient magician Piggiebillah, that the young wife in our Aboriginal legend is unconsciously drawn. At first she places her trust in Piggiebillah's abilities to heal; yet when she becomes aware that this miraculous cure indicates that the old woman is a wirreenun, fear enters her thoughts, and she retreats to the safety of her familiar society.

The real drama in this legend is the conflict between the drives toward cohesion and socialization and the drives toward isolation and individualization. The young wife is caught between these extremes. Upon her escape, she is instructed by the tribe on how to blind the archetypal drive toward individualization until she understands the manner in which it is to be integrated into life. In Aboriginal tradition, bones are used as powerful tools for projection of psychic energies. They are used in this Dreamtime story as a means of protection for the young wife who, with these in hand, pierces the eyes of the old Piggiebillah. The tribe, representing the solidarity of society, enter into the slaying of Piggiebillah, who is transformed eternally into the porcupine. The blinded eyes of Piggiebillah, which become the characteristic deep-set eyes of the porcupine, represent the preoccupation with introspection that is a necessary component of a life of solitude. The porcupine's quills are transformed from the spears of social alienation that the hermit, artist, or mystic must endure. In other words, this social alienation becomes the armor that protects the sort of life experiences in which inner growth is achieved through isolation and austerity.

The onset of menopause marks a natural biological opportunity in a woman's life for her to experience the prototype of the wise woman or hermit. The male derivation of this originally menopausal archetype, celebrated in the monastic renunciation and asceticism, became the spiritual pinnacle of most monotheistic religions. The Christian world absorbed these spiritual values from the transcendental and world-denying doctrines of some Eastern sources, consequently leading to the split between spirituality and ordinary life. The cultural wisdom of the Aborigines avoided this dualism by integrating the hermetic healer archetype into the socialization process.

The archetype of the solitary magically empowered female was the object of the witch hunts of medieval Europe. These atrocities, in which millions of women were tortured and murdered over four centuries, were the result of the Christian church's fear of feminine powers and its attempts to destroy the healing and occult tradition of older women. The female role of sorcerer or healer, handed down through generations, was nearly eradicated during this horrendous period in human history.

The onslaught by the male-dominant society against this female archetype continues today. We can witness this in the range of synthetic hormonal treatments that effectively eliminate the natural processes of menopause. These predominantly male-created pharmaceuticals provide relief for many women whose procreative functions have already been interfered with, and imbalanced by, chemical and mechanical contraceptions. Menopause is a natural stage in a woman's life, and in ancient cultures its suffering was considered an initiation into a deeper, more compassionate knowledge. It was believed that menstrual blood (often thought of as "magic") was retained in the body for nurturing wisdom and vision.[5] Menopause provided a time for a woman to regather, reevaluate, and retrieve the focus of her consciousness from her progeny in preparation for the solitary journey at the end of life. In Aboriginal culture, older women were spiritual authorities and were held in esteem, even by the men of high degree.

The female breast, in many cultures, is a focal point for both erotic and esoteric power.[6] The severing of the young wife's breast signifies withdrawal or transformation of the sexual and erotic aspects of life. Stimulation of the breasts is known to begin lubrication of the vagina, and the suckling of the breast by an infant not only acts as a form of birth control but also contributes to the healing of the womb after childbirth.[7] This aloof, healing, female archetype comes into play in Aboriginal life when women may withdraw from sexual activities for one to two years after childbirth. This not only allows for healing of the internal organs but also is seen as a way in which the female regains her sense of self; it is, for women, one of the advantages of male polygamy.

In our times the continuing repression of the sexual, magical, and spiritual female energies can be seen both metaphysically and biologically as a contributing factor in the rise of breast cancer among women. On a collective level, Carl Jung pointed out that archetypal energies that are suppressed or banished eventually rise in their darkest forms. Similarly, Wilheim Reich documented cases in which the suppression of sexual or emotional energies could be directly related to the development of cancerous growths or tumors. Metaphorically, the severed breast represented the female hermit detached from the socially accepted role of nurturer. In contemporary society, the severed breast appears in its negative form, spreading its shadow across many women's lives as breasts are surgically removed because of cancer or cut open and stuffed with silicone implants in order to fit a stereotypical, male concept of feminine beauty.

Our society does not recognize the archetypal influences in our daily existence; however, in the Aboriginal view of reality, everything has symbolic meaning or nothing has meaning. Every aspect or form of experience is a vehicle for hidden connotations, revealing an interwoven enduring pattern that includes all of humanity and nature. An important aspect of the initiation of a young Aboriginal girl is to develop the sensibilities and concentration that make her aware of the living and symbolic interrelatedness of the natural world. During her isolation she is instructed to listen to the first note that any bird sings throughout the day, to which she must respond with a particular ringing sound. The birds are believed to be inhabited by the spirits of her deceased female ancestors, and in this way a subliminal communication is maintained between the generations. Likewise, she is to focus her attention so that she is aware of every sound made by members of her tribe in their distant camp. This practice of turning full attention to, and filling herself with, the sounds, smells, and sights of her natural and social surroundings is believed to increase the life force and animation of her body. If she does not acquire this capacity to fill herself with the spirit and life of her ambiance, she is told her hair will gray early, her eyes will dull, and her body will soon become limp.[8] In other words, aging to the Aborigines results from a loss of connection with the spirit of earthly life, and it is this deep sense of relatedness and connectivity that must be reawakened if we are to return to environmental sanity and balance.

ENDNOTES

1. K. Langloh Parker, *The Euahlayi Tribe: A Study of Aboriginal Life in Australia* (London: Constable, 1905), 56–57.
2. Ron Vanderwal, ed., *The Aboriginal Photographs of Baldwin Spencer* (Victoria, Australia: Viking O'Neil, 1987), 100–102.
3. Max S. Shapiro and Rhoda A. Hendricks, *A Dictionary of Mythologies* (London: Paladin Books, 1981), 11.
4. Ibid., 11.
5. Barbara Walker, *The Crone* (San Francisco: Harper & Row, 1985), 49.
6. It is widely recognized that the breast is biologically capable of emitting a clear secretion other than milk. In numerous cultures it was understood that these secretions enabled older women, often postmenopausal, to suckle an infant who was not their own. Rufus C. Camphausen, *The Encyclopedia of Erotic Wisdom* (Rochester, Vt.: Inner Traditions International, 1991), 27.
7. Robert Anton Wilson, *Ishtar Rising,* (Las Vegas: Falcon Press, 1989), 27.
8. Parker, *The Euahlayi Tribe,* 57.

THE RAINBIRD

Boogoo-doo-ga-da was an old woman who lived alone with her four hundred dingoes. From living so long with these dogs, she had grown not to care for her fellow creatures except as food. She and the dogs lived on human flesh, and it was her cunning that gained such food for them all.

She would sally forth from her camp with her two little dogs; she would be sure to meet some blackfellows, probably twenty or thirty, going down to the creek. She would say, "I can tell you where there are lots of Mai-ras [paddymelons, a type of wallaby]."

They would ask where, and she would answer, "Over there, on the point of that morilla [pebbly ridge]. If you will go there and have your nullas [clubs] ready, I will go with my two little dogs and round them up toward you."

The blackfellows invariably stationed themselves where she had told them, and off went Boogoo-doo-ga-da and her two dogs. But not to round up the Mai-ras.

She went quickly toward her camp, calling softly, "Birri gu gu," which meant "Sool'em, sool'em" and was the signal for the dingoes to come out.

Quickly they came and surrounded the blackfellows, took

them by surprise, flew at them, bit them, and worried them to death.

Then they and Boogoo-doo-ga-da dragged the bodies to their camp. There they were cooked and were food for the old woman and the dogs for some time. As soon as the supply was finished, the process was repeated.

The blackfellows missed so many of their friends that they determined to find out what had become of them. They began to suspect the old woman who lived alone and hunted over the morillas with her two little dogs. They proposed that the next party that went to the creek should divide and some stay behind in hiding and watch what went on.

Those watching saw the old woman advance toward their friends, talk to them for a while, and then go off with her two dogs. They saw their friends station themselves at the point of the morilla, holding their nullas in readiness, as if waiting for something to come. Presently, they heard a low cry from the old woman of "Birri gu gu," which cry was quickly followed by dingoes coming out of the bush in every direction, in hundreds, surrounding the blackfellows at the point.

The dingoes closed in, quickly hemming the blackfellows in all round; then they made a simultaneous rush at them, tore them with their teeth, and killed them.

The blackfellows watching saw that when the dingoes had killed their friends, they were joined by the old woman, who helped them to drag off the bodies to their camp.

Having seen all this, back went the watchers to their tribe and told what they had seen.

All the tribes around mustered up and decided to execute a swift vengeance.

In order to do so, out they sallied well armed. A detachment went on to entrap the dingoes and Boogoo-doo-ga-da. Then just when the usual killing of the blacks was to begin and the dingoes were closing in round them for the purpose, up rushed over two hundred blackfellows, and so successful was their attack that every little dingo was killed, as well as Boogoo-doo-ga-da and her two little dogs.

The old woman lay where she had been slain, but as the blacks went away, they heard her cry, "Boogoo-doo-ga-da."

So back they went and broke her bones; first they broke her legs and then left her. But again as they went they heard her cry "Boogoo-doo-ga-da."So back they came, and again, until at last every bone in her body was broken, but still she cried, "Boogoo-doo-ga-da." So one man waited beside her to see whence came the sound, for surely, they thought, she must be dead. He saw her heart move and cry again, "Boogoo-doo-ga-da," and as it cried, out came a little bird from it.

This little bird runs on the morillas and calls at night, "Boogoo-doo-ga-da." All day it stays in one place, and only at night it comes out. It is a little grayish bird, something like a weeday or bowerbird. The blacks call it a rain-maker, for if anyone steals its eggs, it cries out incessantly, "Boogoo-doo-ga-da," until in answer to its call the rain falls. And when the country is stricken with a drought, the Daens look for one of these little birds and, finding it, chase it until it cries aloud, "Boogoo-doo-ga-da," and when they hear its cry in the day-time, they know the rain will soon fall.

As the little bird flew from the heart of the woman, all the dead dingoes were changed into snakes of many different kinds, all poisonous. The two little dogs were changed into Daya-minya, a very small kind of carpet snake, nonpoisonous, for these two little dogs had never bitten the Daens as the other dingoes had done. At the points of the morillas, where Boogoo-doo-ga-da and her dingoes used to slay the blacks, are heaps of white stones, which are supposed to be the fossilized bones of the men she killed.

 COMMENTARY

The Aborigines have often been accused of, or associated with, the practice of cannibalism; documentation indicates, however, that the partaking of human flesh was done in an infrequent, limited, and ritualistic manner. On the other hand, the theme of cannibalism threaded through many of the Aboriginal legends suggests their predominantly symbolic understanding and utilization of this practice. In this story of the Rainbird, we meet the Ancestor Boogoo-doo-ga-da, who traps and devours that which she has shunned, or been rejected by—the kinship of her tribal people.

The joyous, intimate, and complex web of tribal life, which the hermit Boogoo-doo-ga-da was denied, ensures that each person's needs for food and human interaction are fulfilled. In this context, her cannibalism represents the unconscious mechanisms through which we invariably satisfy unacknowledged or denied needs and desires. Boogoo-doo-ga-da's devouring of the groups of male hunters symbolizes the way we compulsively consume, from the world around us, in order to feed our inner sense of inadequacy, deprivation, self-denial, or lack of self-esteem.

Although the contemporary world feels revulsion toward cannibalism and outlaws it on a physical level, its psychological and psychic forms are rampant among us. Competition and commercialism particularly seduce us into believing that our repressed or thwarted dreams or desires can be filled by behaving as, resembling, or consuming a host of stereotypes. We are conditioned to desire not only the stockings but also the legs of the model in the stocking advertisement, the biceps of the super sports hero, or the face of the Hollywood movie star. For perhaps 150,000 years, before the advent of modern civilization, humanity lived as tribal hunters and gatherers. Psychologist Robert Johnson speculates that much of our behavior reflects dark, disturbed aspects of our long repressed and denied tribal consciousness, of which the transformation of ritual cannibalism into the contemporary frenzy of psychic and psychological feeding is a good example.

This modern, commercialized, sublimated form of cannibalism is reminiscent of, yet vastly different from, such behavior as it was expressed in indigenous culture. For example, in Aboriginal culture, a younger tribal man might ingest a portion of the thigh of a highly accomplished deceased hunter in order to assimilate some of his great skills, or at the death of an elder, the body fluids might be ingested or rubbed onto one's skin in order to partake of the essential qualities of the revered person.[1] Aboriginal cannibalism, in this regard, occurred only within the context of a natural death and was not associated with the later versions from other cultures, which included human sacrifice. For the Aborigines, the sacred physical act of cannibalism was concurrent with deep, sympathetic states of consciousness in which not only was a psychological identity established, but also a powerful psychic vibration was imparted and exchanged.[2] Cannibalism, in this sense, denotes interchange of a quality or energy between beings who have entered into a deep, metaphysical rapport. By being unaware of the psychic and ritual mechanisms that this process involves, our society is left with an infantile and commercially exploited inversion of cannibalism.

The Aborigines do not moralize on the enslavement of human nature by unconscious or unsatiated desires, which Boogoo-doo-ga-da represents. Rather, they acknowledge that through her symbolic death and rebirth these dangerous and antisocial qualities are transformed. The tenaciousness of the appetites of human nature is indicated by the fact that the men of the tribe return numerous times to break Boogoo-doo-ga-da's bones. However, this dark insatiable drive of Boogoo-doo-ga-da is transformed and finally leaps from her heart in the form of a little rainbird. In other words, the corrupt excesses of Boogoo-doo-ga-da give birth to their opposite: a force of purification that brings cleansing rains.

K. Langloh Parker mentions the time of a severe drought when a rainbird entered her garden, and, upon hearing its cry, the Aborigines claimed rain would fall. Soon after, it poured. During another drought, when the Aboriginal rainmakers were unable to burst the pregnant clouds and make the sky stream with rain, some of the older Aborigines saw a rainbird and chased it. Unfortunately, that time they were unable to make it call out, and the drought continued.[3]

Within many archaic legends there are female goddesses who, like Boogoo-doo-ga-da, are accompanied by dogs and, in all cases, are associated with death. The faithful wolflike dogs of Hel, the Nordic underworld goddess, help her escort the dead to the next world, and, like Boogoo-doo-ga-da's dingoes, they nip the flesh of the corpses. The dog aspect of this myth also resonates in some funeral customs of India, in which dogs are ritually offered a morsel of the dead body.[4] In ancient Egyptian mythology, Anubis, the jackal dog, was the guardian of death and the devourer of the remains of the deceased. Also Hecate, the Queen of Shades, claimed her dog as guardian of the gateway to the realm of Hades, the world between life and death.[5] In this Aboriginal legend, Boogoo-doo-ga-da is symbolic of the metaphysical meaning of cannibalism; that is, in the guise of death, the universal creation devours itself.

Dogs were the protectors of the huntress goddess Artemis, again representing the feminine isolated from society and adversarial to the detached, exclusively male role of hunter. The male god Actaeon's unwanted penetration into the feminine mysteries and the wilderness angered the goddess, who turned Actaeon into a stag and thus incited his own dogs to destroy him.[6]

In this myth, the dingoes are a projection of Boogoo-doo-ga-da's hunger for the masculine energy that she shunned. Following their dark feast, the dingoes turned into snakes, often a symbol of the assimilation or co-mingling of the masculine and feminine energies. In myths throughout the world, analogically, snakes and dogs are both associated with the feminine and are synonymous in that each possesses the power to dwell in the intermediary worlds between life and death. For example, the half-human goddesses named the Erinyes were symbolized by both dogs and snakes.[7] The sensual snake that mysteriously sheds its skin embodies the continual balance of death and rebirth. The ancient symbol of the snake devouring its own tail (the "uroborus") represents the universal interdependency of opposites: hunger/satiation, life/death, female/male.

In the death and rebirth of the female Ancestor Boogoo-doo-ga-da, a seemingly simple Aboriginal narrative has precisely touched symbolic combinations that appeared and persisted through the myths of most cultures and ages.

ENDNOTES

1. K. Langloh Parker, *The Euahlayi Tribe: A Study of Aboriginal Life in Australia* (London: Constable, 1905), 38.

2. Christian missionaries supposedly put an end to these forms of ritual practices.
3. Parker, *The Euahlayi Tribe,* 101.
4. Buffie Johnson, *Lady of the Beasts* (San Francisco: Harper & Row, 1988), 117.
5. Ibid.
6. Jean Shinoda Bolen, M.D., *Goddesses in Every Woman* (New York: Harper & Row, 1984), 48.
7. Johnson, 117.

THREE

TALES OF THE MAGICAL POWERS

That which is subtle, ambiguous, interconnected, intangible, and beyond reason or logic emerges from the realms of the Universal Feminine and is the basis of what has been called "magic" or "the occult." This dimension of existence, so long banished from an active, formative role in our worldview, is revealed in these legends as fundamental and sacred to the framework of humanity's oldest culture, the Australian Aborigines.

MOODOOBAHNGUL, THE WIDOW

Moodoobahngul, a widow, was living at Nagerbeyah with her two little children, a boy and a girl.

One night the two little children began to cry for durrie (grass-seed bread), for they were hungry.

Their mother told them to stop crying, but they would not, and at last she called to frighten them, "Marmbeyah! Marmbeyah!" a name sometimes given to Minggah, or tree spirits.

"Marmbeyah! Where have you all got to? These children will not cease crying."

To her surprise, the Marmbeyah answered, "Wait, wait. Give us time to get to you. You know we are very old; we shall stumble over those sticks lying about if we hurry."

When Moodoobahngul heard them answer, she was frightened. She had not meant the spirits to come, she had but wished to quiet her children. She now seized hold of her boy and girl, took them into her dardurr (bark shelter), and hid them in a corner under the opossum rug; then she went and sat by the fire as if by herself.

As she heard the tap, tapping of the Marmbeyah's yam-sticks getting closer, she armed herself with a murroomon, a stick having at the end a piece of sharpened emu leg bone.

When the Marmbeyah were all round her fire, and one came toward her as if to enter the dardurr where her children were hidden, Moodoobahngul stuck the point of the murroomon into his eye.

"Mildee, mildee, girro doorungnee widya gurrhgay, werhurrah goognee goalarh gurrahgingnee goalarh gurrahgingnee, "which means, "My eye, my eye, it is hit. Speak, what is the matter, what is wrong?"

The Marmbeyah thought a trap had been laid for them. They had but answered the call of the woman for them, and this was the treatment that awaited them. It was surely a trap. They would not stay to walk away but, using their spirit power, rose into the air and passed back to their Minggah, where they knew they were safe.

 COMMENTARY

The Aborigines believe that the spirits of the newborn have a complete conscious preexistence in what is referred to as the Realm of the Unborn.[1] Through a combination of psychic and natural forces and events (which are not dependent upon, but may include, sexual intercourse between parents), the preexistent spirit of the child is brought into the physical world of the living.

The marvelous transition made by infants from the womb into the spacious physical world is concurrent with the passage from the depths of their spirit origin to that of living consciousness. The Aborigines believe that children, by nature, are in touch with the unseen world and that they remain divided between the spirit realms and physical embodiment for several years before they are completely conjoined with the natural world. For this reason, knowledge of the spirit world is of utmost significance to mothers, who must nurture and communicate with the spiritual energies of their children throughout the process of their physical maturation.

This story discusses some of the knowledge and understanding of the spirit world that Aboriginal women use in child rearing. K. Langloh Parker points out that Euahlayi women believe that children can see spirits invisible to others and that when children smile or crow to themselves, they are really communicating with the spirits. The Aborigines explain the typical behavior of infants opening and closing their hands by saying that the baby's spirit is still wandering with the spirit clan, hunting, gathering, and, particularly, "catching crabs" in the Realm of the Unborn.[2]

The legend of Moodoobahngul is a reminder or warning to mothers that the spirit energy is close at hand and easily provoked from the atmosphere surrounding a child. Birthing rituals emphasize this presence of psychic forces. For example, when a woman is about to give birth, the grandmother will often try to tempt the unborn into the new world. However, when the mother feels the pangs of labor beginning, the child will often playfully decline the over-anxious request of the grandmother and will not appear unless she remains a "silent spectator." It is then left to another female kin to entice the child out of the nurturing womb. Very often the female kin will begin this ritual with descriptions of all the people who are so anxious to meet the unborn, such as auntie, sister, father's sister, and many more, saying, for example, "Come now, here's your auntie waiting to see you." If these numerous attempts fail, the enticer will begin to report on the bountiful fruits that are in season or a glorious place that is waiting to be visited by the newborn: "Make haste, the bumble fruit is ripe. The guiebet flowers are blooming. The grass is waving high. The birds are all talking. And it is a beautiful place, hurry up and see for yourself."

Often, however, the baby is considered too smart to be tempted to leave such a warm sanctuary, so an older wise woman present at the birth will brandish a wi-mouyan, or clever stick. She waves this wand over the expectant mother and resisting child, crooning a charm as she does so.[3] The baby, under the spell of the clever woman, then emerges into the light of the natural world. This and many other accounts exemplify how Aboriginal women communicate with the pre-born as fully comprehending, intelligent beings and illustrates that communication between the living and the unborn always includes an awareness of psychic factors at play. This ancient ritual is also reflected in the activities of many contemporary psychologists, who have shown great interest in the intellectual responses and memory of the unborn.[4]

Among the Euahlayi people, the spiritual formation of babies begins under the auspices of Bahloo the moon—in the case of female babies, in collaboration with Wahn the crow. From a stone, or goomarh, sacred to Bahloo, the female spirits are propelled toward their prospective parents. Bahloo assists the wood lizard, Boomayahmayahmul, in the formation of male babies. During conception, the sperm of the father acts as an agent in preparing the womb and facilitating the deposit of a child's spirit within the mother to be. However, psychic forces in certain places such as trees, rocks, or water holes, not the sperm, are considered to be the causative components in the impregnation. A child born without direct involvement by a father is considered a "spirit child" and can sometimes be recognized by having teeth when born. A spirit child may be sent to Waddahgudjaelwon (a birth-giving spirit), who dispatches it to hang "promiscuously" off the Coolabah trees. These baby spirits then seize a prospective mother as she passes underneath the tree. Another possibility for a spirit child to enter a woman is through the action of the Wurrawilberoo, whom we encountered in another context in the legend of Bralgah. The Wurrawilberoo are said to snatch up a baby spirit and, clothing it in a whirlwind, race it toward the woman in whom they wish it to incarnate.[5]

When a spirit child is born, it is believed to have a Coolabah leaf in its mouth, and an old woman present at the birth must take this Coolabah leaf from the newborn's mouth in order to ensure that the baby will not return to the spiritland, or Realm of the Unborn.[6]

In some cases, the blood of disappointed child spirits who have been unsuccessful in capturing a mother will be transformed into the orange-red flowers of mistletoe branches. Always, however, the spirits of babies or children who die young will be returned to an eathly existence and will be able to choose either their original mother (being called *millanboo*, the same again) or, if they so desire, a different woman. [7]

In addition to the Coolabah tree as a habitat for unborn children, trees in general play an important role in the birth-giving process. Often an Aboriginal woman in labor will squat against the trunk of a tree. In several other indigenous cultures, women are tied to, or hold onto, a tree during the birthing process. The sturdy strength and upright body of the tree create a solid support for women as they undergo a life-death initiation into the feminine mysteries. While all males, including the father, are disallowed from attending the birth, the phallic symbolism of the tree represents the presence of the Universal Masculine, as well as the animus, or masculine energy, within the female.[8] In the Aboriginal worldview, natural forms such as trees express characteristics that are qualities of either the Universal Masculine or the Universal Feminine. The ancient practice of allocating gender to things in one's surroundings has been retained in the grammar of many modern languages.

In this legend the tree spirits are again symbolic of the masculine, this time being called to assist in disciplining the children of the widowed Moodoobahngul. However, Moodoobahngul soon realizes her mistake in using the spirits as a threat. In traditional Aboriginal culture, children, up until adolescence, are tended almost exclusively by the tribal women. While the masculine tendencies to aggressively control, limit, and punish are of positive value in other aspects of Aboriginal social order, they have no part in child rearing.

According to K. Langloh Parker, Aboriginal mothers are extremely cautious with the type of spirits they wish to attract to their children, just as Aboriginal society is extremely cautious in handling the fragile innocence and disposition or temperament of infants. The women are not only constantly attentive to their children's physical needs but also alert to messages and warnings from the psychic and spiritual worlds. The Aborigines attribute the unpredictable and often seemingly unprovoked reactions that are the hallmark of infant behavior all over the world to the spiritual entities always in close proximity to children.

Massage is an important tool in coping with the strong spiritual energy within children's bodies. Children with difficulty sleeping may have their skulls and foreheads rubbed with a form of pollen from a needlebush tree in order to remove the troubling spirit. During the night, when young children awake, mothers will often warm their hands and then rub their babies' limbs, spine, or joints. This engenders a harmonious spiritual flow and therefore creates suppleness and fine proportions in the children when grown. When children are distressed and their crying continues unabated, powerful negative spirits are considered to dwell within them. An antidote is to "smoke" the babies by holding them over a thick, smoking fire of burning budtha twigs.

During children's sleeping hours, mothers constantly check their mouths, making certain that they are shut and that they are breathing through their noses. This is to prevent a "bad" spirit from slipping a disease or negative energy in through a child's tiny mouth. Similarly, babies are not allowed to lie on their backs unless their heads are covered. In the unusual instance of a gilah bird flying over the camp at night, crying as it passes, young children are turned on their left sides to avoid any evil consequences. If the velvet-black, cawing crow flies over the camp at night, children are laid on their right sides. Neither of these birds is usually active at night, and therefore their presence indicates a suspicious energy abroad in bird form.[9]

Contemporary women have little or no recourse to the psychic or spiritual levels of child rearing. Instead, we are conditioned to raise children by the dictates of external conditions and the purely rational mind, and rather than seeing children as sensitive receivers of the flux and flow of a spirited milieu, their behavior is blamed on individual character.

ENDNOTES

1. Robert Lawlor, *Voices of the First Day: Awakening in the Aboriginal Dreamtime* (Rochester, Vt.: Inner Traditions International, 1991), 179.
2. K. Langloh Parker, *The Euahlayi Tribe: A Study of Aboriginal Australia* (London: Constable, 1905), 46.
3. Ibid., 40.
4. Contemporary psychology has recently become aware of the "pre-birth" consciousness of the unborn, and extensive research is being carried out on "pre-birth" memory. In the Aboriginal ritual the child requires enticing into its new domain. John Richard and Troye Turner, "Round Pegs in Round (W)Holes," in *The Whole Person* magazine (Hurstbridge, Victoria, Australia, October/November 1991).
5. Ibid., 51–52.
6. Ibid., 52.
7. Ibid., 51.
8. Sylvia Brinton Perera, *Descent to the Goddess* (Toronto: Inner City Books, 1981), 39.
9. Parker, *The Euahlayi Tribe,* 53.

THE WIRREENUN MOTHER
AND HER WIRREENUN SON

A mother and her son and her son's wife were all traveling together. The wife was not well at the time, and the son said, "You two go straight on to the creek, close to the old yaraan [white gum tree]. I will go around and get some opossums and honey, then meet you there when you get a fire ready."

Off he started. His mother and wife went toward the place he had named, stopping every now and then to dig yams until they had a good quantity.

The wife was tired and glad indeed when they reached the old yaraan. But, tired as she was, she helped her mother-in-law to dig a hole, make a fire in it, put some stones on the fire, then, when the stones were heated and the fire burnt down, lay some leaves and grass on it and then the yams, over which they placed more grass and sprinkled water, then more grass and a thick coating of earth, leaving the yams to cook. While the yams were cooking, they made a bough shade, and the old mother said to the young wife: "You are tired. Lie down here in the shade, and I'll tease your hair. It will take the pain out of your head and make you sleep."

The young wife lay down, and the old woman sat beside her and teased her hair, which soon soothed her off to sleep.

When the old woman judged from her breathing that she
was asleep, she made sure by touching her on the eyes; still
she breathed heavily. Then she touched her mouth; still she
breathed heavily. Then she touched her nose; still she breathed
heavily, so she must be sound asleep.

The old mother caught hold tightly of both the girl's wrists
and, leaning over her, drove her front teeth right into the
middle of her face, biting a piece off.

The young wife woke with a start and cried aloud, but the
old mother had her fast.

The unstanched blood poured forth, and the young wife died.

The old mother carried her to the creek, where she had a
Minggah (spirit tree), for she was a wirreenun, or witch.

In the meantime, the husband, who likewise was a
wirreenun, had a warning that his wife was in danger. He
determined to be content with what opossums and honey he
had and hurried on to the appointed meeting place, feeling
sure that some calamity was happening to his wife.

As he neared the place, he saw the bough shade. "Ah!" he
said, "they are all right."

But when he reached there, he saw neither of the women.
He saw where they had the yams baking. He threw down his
own spoils and looked round.

He saw a trail of little black ants going to the bough shade.
He looked in, and there was blood. He tracked that blood until
near the Minggah. He then heard his mother's voice, first
laughing, then singing. He heard her rejoicing over the good
feed of flesh she was having, secure, as she thought, in her
hollow Minggah. The son felt rage burn within him as he heard
her laughing over her victim, his much-loved young wife, who
he had hoped would soon be the mother of his son.

He went back to the scrub—he gathered some pine bark and
some beebuyer, or broom bushes. These he carried to the
Minggah, beside which was a hole. Into this hole he crept and
then set the bark and brush alight.

His mother heard the crackling of the fire under the base of the tree. "My son," she called, "it is your mother here. Your own mother. Put out that fire."

"I will not put out the fire. What has my mother done with my young wife? What is she doing with her now?"

"But my son, I am your mother. You must care for your mother and save her from burning."

Crackle, crackle went the pine bark; the Minggah was soon on fire.

"I cared more for my young wife. Where is she? Can you give me back my young wife, she who was soon to be the mother of my son? No, you cannot, so burn, burn."

He poked the fire into a brighter flame, and it crackled again.

"But, my son, I know this is a Minggah. Evil will befall you if you injure a Minggah or anyone touching one. Surely the spirits will kill you. Stay that fire ere it be too late."

"No harm will come to me. Only at a goomarh [spirit-haunted stone] would you be safe from my vengeance, for I, though you knew it not, am a wirreenun and a greater one than you. To me no harm will come—to you only. To you who killed my young wife—she who was to be the mother of my son. To you who ate her flesh—the flesh of the wife your son loved. Burn! Burn! Burn!"

He sang aloud a wirreenun's song. The flames leapt up the tree, enveloping his mother and the remains of his young wife, which were burned together. Then, with sorrow in his breast for the loss of his young wife and joy that, though his mother had been a wirreenun, he had been a greater one and so able to avenge that loss, he went on his solitary way.

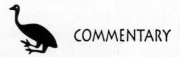

COMMENTARY

Between the ages of eleven and thirteen years, a young Aborigine boy begins a series of initiations called by the Aborigines "the making of a man." These puberty initiations, the first of which often involves circumcision, are representative of the continual death and rebirth processes necessary for the shedding of one stage of life and the embracing of a new. One important aspect of these male puberty rites is the altering of the mother-son relationship, which changes from one of great affection and intimacy to one of formal restraint and distance. These initiations serve a dual purpose: the severing of the potentially incestuous bond between a boy and his mother that could later restrain or inhibit his ability to have a mature sexual relationship with other women, as well as releasing the woman from the demanding stage in her life of the nurturing, supporting mother.

The severance of the mother-son bond also allows the male to enter the world of men and male initiations in which maternal dependency is transformed into a mature bond with the Universal Feminine, "the mother earth," who will be his new guide and provider. The primary relationship of child to parent is transformed into one of great intimacy between himself as hunter and all of the natural world. K. Langloh Parker comments on the depth of communication between hunter and wild creature: "They say a fully initiated man can sing a charm which will make a piggiebillah relax his grip and be taken without any trouble."[1]

Early in this myth the young man ventures off hunting, signifying he has developed his capacities as hunter and communer with the natural world. However, his translation into manhood is not fully completed, because, against his kinship code, he has lingered too long in a close relationship with his mother. What the Aborigines term "remaining in the shadow of the mother" is the dramatic flaw of this tragic story. The gruesome result of the infraction of this cultural law is the destruction of the young man's wife and the possibilities of her conceiving their child, as well as the torching and subsequent burning to death of his murderous and devouring mother.

In our culture, the Oedipus myth was chosen by Freud to represent the battleground of incestuous drives and psychological and psychic entwinements involved in the mother-son relationship. This personal psychological phenomenon is seen by many to be a chronic underlying condition of our entire civilization. In his epic film *Best Intentions,* the great Swedish filmmaker Ingmar Bergman explores the subject of incest within European society between mother and son, father and daughter, mother and daughter, father and son, and sister and brother. As a result of Christianity's assault on ancient traditions, the true basis of initiatic culture, which involved transference of secret knowledge and laws through definite stages and progressions in life and consciousness, was lost. Previous to Christianity, these cultures effectively dissolved, at adolescence, an initiate's bonds with the nuclear family and expanded the young person's sense of belonging and relatedness to the entire natural world as well as to the vastly extended kinship system. In place of this form of cultural transmission from generation to generation, European society conveyed continuity and order predominantly through the complex patterns of incest (fixated, unconsciously charged family relationships) and the bequeathing of possessions and ownership. Through ceremonial enactment and social restrictions, the Aborigines ensure that potential patterns of incest are transformed into an intimate engagement with nature and metaphysical law. It is their belief that unless the individual passes through the death of the child-parent and sibling relationships, no other transitions or separations in life, including one's own death, can be accomplished with a clear spiritual vision or deep understanding.

Within this myth, the detailed description of the important cooking technique of baking yams is an example of a practical layer of information woven into this otherwise symbolic narrative. In traditional life, cooking would customarily be performed by the young wife. That the old mother, on this occasion, usurps the young wife's position can be interpreted as a signal of her hungering urge to displace the younger woman. The old mother chooses to soothe the young wife into a state of repose by teasing her hair—an action that has powerful implications on a psychic level. Hair, to the Aborigines, is a potent transmitter of subtle energies for both healing and sorcery. The Aborigines believe that if a lock of a person's hair falls into the hands of a wirreenun, or sorcerer, who wishes to perform "bad magic" on that person, death is imminent.

The pattern now beginning to reveal itself is of the old mother draining energy from the young wife and reabsorbing the love that the son has attached to his wife. This vampirism suddenly shifts from the realms of the psychic into the physical. The three strategies of the old mother in sensing the young wife's breathing represent the three "doorways of perception"— that is, a progression from the most external perceptual mode, the eyes, to the mouth and then to the nose. The nose in all esoteric traditions is the deepest sensor that conveys information directly to the limbic system or inner brain. When finally the old mother believes she has lulled the young

wife into a deep sleep, she strikes the middle of the young wife's face with
her front teeth, penetrating her third eye, the center of inner vision. There
is no longer hope for the young wife; the irreversible devouring by the dark
and destructive mother has begun.

The image of this dark mother conjures, on a cosmic level, the Hindu
goddess Kali, who is "representative of both fertility and time, a personifi-
cation of the opposing forces of creation and destruction."[2] In this story, the
young man hears his mother laughing; so, too, the goddess Kali laughs as
she devours the corpse upon which she is pictured standing, showing her
dreadful teeth and creating a fearful vision as she "expresses her dominion
over all that exists." Yet, in this devouring, this destruction, there is hope
and joy.[3] When all is destroyed and the irreversible procession of time or
cycles is appeased, the true nature of the dark, devouring mother reveals
itself as the power that removes a completed cycle in order for a new birth
and a new creation to occur.

The archetypal pattern of Kali as creator and devourer of all life is
symbolized in the deeply sacred Aboriginal ritual of the eating of a dead
person's flesh, discussed earlier in "The Rainbird." In traditional tribal life
it was claimed that there was nothing more strengthening, either physically
or mentally, than this ancient ceremony. A ritual similar to this was
described by K. Langloh Parker: "Before a body was placed into a bark
coffin, a few incisions were made in it; when it was coffined it was stood
on end, and what drained from the incisions was caught in small wirrees
[drinking vessels] and drunk by the mourners."[4]

The English word to describe this sacred ceremony is "cannibalism,"
which, to the Western mind, holds many shuddering connotations and
images of "savages" tearing pieces off other humans merely for material
sustenance. To the Aborigines, this process holds psychic, psychological,
and physical meaning connected to both black and white magic. The
Aboriginal culture, being the oldest, sheds understanding on the symbolism of cannibalistic ritual, which has been incorporated in many religious
traditions through the eons. The Aborigines believed the living were
empowered by the transmuting juices or essence of the newly deceased.
Reciprocally, the dead were able to spread their life force, through their
kin, in the sense of perpetuating their essence. In Dionysian rituals, a
spiritual state of divine life is believed to be achieved through participation
in a meal of the flesh of the god himself; and the "mystery religions of the

early Christian era centered on a pseudo-cannibalistic sacrament believed to identify the worshipper with the worshipped."[5] In many ancient cultures, including the Egyptian, Mexican, and Aztecan, ritual cannibalism represented rebirth, while in others it was said to strengthen kinship bonds and allow women to conceive more easily.[6]

Both the Minggah tree, in which the old mother takes refuge, and the spirit-haunted goomarh stone that is mentioned at the end of the story play essential roles in Aboriginal culture. K. Langloh Parker claims she is reminded of these two sacred elements by a saying attributed to Christ: "Raise the stone, and there thou shalt find me; cleave the wood and there am I." A Minggah is a spirit-animated tree that is chosen by a wirreenun woman or man as a place of refuge in times of danger and with which the wirreenun has a complex and sacred relationship. The health and magical ability of the wirreenun is often dependent upon the condition of the Minggah. Such was the empathetic relationship wirreenuns had with their sacred trees or stones that if anything happened to them, they would become ill and sometimes die. While people may seek refuge during times of danger at a Minggah tree, they must be prepared for the wrath of the tree spirits, as both the Minggah tree and the goomarh, or sacred stone, are taboo to all but their own wirreenuns.[8] Only highly initiated wirreenuns have a goomarh, and unlike the Minggah, these are impenetrable to all others.[9]

Fire, often used symbolically as a transformative element in these Aboriginal tales, is for the son the generator of a new life. As our story closes, his heart center is sorrowful yet free from the oppressive bondage of his mother. Innocence and purity have been sacrificed in the form of the young wife, an event that also represents the young man's discovery and appreciation of his own yielding, receptive, inner feminine. His mother, in displaying the negative aspects of the feminine, has also been sacrificed for his manhood, enabling him to confront and survive the inclement depths of the dark feminine.

Some of the themes from this powerful Aboriginal tale not only resonate with other ancient cultures but also parallel certain theories in modern psychology as well. The boundless sense of self-giving and love that an infant boy experiences in his mother's embrace becomes the love that he searches for in his mature life, be it in romantic pursuits or in erotic or spiritual experiences. The young wife or lover is, symbolically, the externalized form of this initial maternal warmth and depth of feeling transformed, through male initiation, into sexual involvement and creativity. In this instance, because of the lingering bond between the young wirreenun and his mother, his mature relationship to the feminine is aborted, as symbolized by the murder of his beloved wife. Today, the same lack of resolve in mother-son relationships creates a society in which sexuality between men and women has ceased to be a doorway to spiritual openings, where erotic intensities and ritual have been lost, and where men, fearful of their unconscious incestual attachment to the mother, direct their feelings of guilt and anger toward the feminine in general. Often the mother, laden with her unconscious attachment to the son, freezes her own sexuality and continues to project her desires upon the son and his lovers.

It is not only the old wirreenun mother in this myth who is guilty of an incestuous attachment, but also the young man, who continues in a childlike manner to draw upon the maternal source. The unappeased, emptied mother represents the supreme void, where all of life is inevitably swallowed into the womb of the dark earth. What nature creates, she must also take back. The young initiated hunter glimpses the depths of this eternal truth in witnessing the murder of his wife and burning of his mother. Symbolically he has looked into the endless destruction of the ineluctable cycles of time. Thus he comes to know that the most frightening darkness is also the source of all light and creation.

ENDNOTES

1. K. Langloh Parker, *The Euahlayi Tribe: A Study of Aboriginal Life in Australia* (London: Constable, 1905), 115.
2. Max S. Shapiro and Rhoda A. Hendricks, *A Dictionary of Mythologies* (London: Paladin Books, 1981), 100.
3. Alain Daniélou, *The Myths and Gods of India* (New York: Inner Traditions International, 1991), 273.
4. Parker, *The Euahlayi Tribe*, 38.
5. Barbara Walker, *The Woman's Encyclopedia of Myths and Secrets* (San Francisco: Harper & Row, 1983), 136.
6. Ibid., 137.
7. Parker, *The Euahlayi Tribe*, 22.
8. Ibid., 36.
9. Ibid., 27.

THE REDBREASTS

Gwai-nee-bu and Goomai the water-rat were down at the creek one day, getting mussels for food, when, to their astonishment, a kangaroo hopped right into the water beside them.

They knew well that it must be escaping from hunters, who were probably pressing it close. So Gwai-nee-bu quickly seized her yamstick and knocked the kangaroo on the head; it was caught fast in the weeds in the creek, so it could not escape.

When the two old women had killed the kangaroo, they hid its body under the weeds in the creek, fearing to take it out and cook it straightaway lest the hunters should come up and claim it. The little son of Gwai-nee-bu watched them from the bank.

After having hidden the kangaroo, the women picked up their mussels and started for their camp, when up came the hunters, Ooya and Gidgerigar, who had tracked the kangaroo right to the creek.

Seeing the women, they said, "Did you see a kangaroo?"

The women answered, "No. We saw no kangaroo."

"That is strange, for we have tracked it right up to here."

"We have seen no kangaroo. See, we have been digging out mussels for food. Come to our camp, and we will give you some when they are cooked."

The young men, puzzled, followed the women to their camp, and when the mussels were cooked, the hunters joined the old women at their dinner.

The little boy would not eat the mussels; he kept crying to his mother, "Gwai-nee-bu, Gwai-nee-bu. I want kangaroo. I want kangaroo. Gwai-nee-bu. Gwai-nee-bu."

"There," said Ooya, "your little boy has seen the kangaroo and wants some; it must be here somewhere."

"Oh, no. He cries for anything he thinks of, some days for kangaroo; he is only a little boy and does not know what he wants," said old Gwai-nee-bu.

But still the child kept saying, "Gwai-nee-bu. Gwai-nee-bu. I want kangaroo. I want kangaroo."

Goomai was so angry with little Gwai-nee-bu for keeping on asking for kangaroo, and thereby making the young men suspicious, that she hit him hard on the mouth to keep him quiet, so that the blood came and trickled down his breast, staining it red. When she saw this, old Gwai-nee-bu grew angry in her turn and hit old Goomai, who returned the blow. And so a fight began, more words than blows; so the noise was great, the women fighting, little Gwai-nee-bu crying, not quite knowing whether he was crying because Goomai hit him, because his mother was fighting, or because he still wanted kangaroo.

Ooya said to Gidgerigar, "They have the kangaroo somewhere hidden; let us slip away now in the confusion. We will only hide, then come back in a little while and surprise them."

They went quietly away, and as soon as the two women noticed they had gone, they ceased fighting and determined to cook the kangaroo. They watched the two young men until they were out of sight and waited some time so as to be sure of their own safety. Then down they hurried to get the kangaroo. They dragged it out and were just making a big fire on which to cook it, when up came Ooya and Gidgerigar, saying,

"Ah! We thought so. You had our kangaroo all the time. Little Gwai-nee-bu was right."

"But we killed it," said the women.

"But we hunted it here," said the men and, so saying, caught hold of the kangaroo and dragged it away some distance, where they made a fire and cooked it.

Goomai, Gwai-nee-bu, and her little boy went over to Ooya and Gidgerigar and begged for some of the meat, but the young men would give them none, though little Gwai-nee-bu cried piteously for some. But no; they said they would rather throw what they did not want to the hawks than give it to the women or child.

At last, seeing that there was no hope of their getting any, the women went away. They built a big dardurr or bark shelter, for themselves, shutting themselves and the little boy up in it. Then they began singing a song that was to invoke a storm to destroy their enemies, for so now they considered Ooya and Gidgerigar. So for some time they chanted:

> Mooharah, Moogaray, May May
> Eehu, Eehu, Doon-gara.

Which means:

> Hailstones, hailstones, wind, wind,
> Rain, rain, lightning.

They would begin very slowly and softly, gradually getting quicker and louder, until at length they almost shrieked it out.

While they were chanting, little Gwai-nee-bu kept crying and would not be comforted. Soon came a few big drops of rain, then a big wind, and as that lulled, more rain. Then came thunder and lightning, the air grew bitterly cold, and there came a pitiless hailstorm. Hailstones bigger than a duck's egg fell, cutting the leaves from the trees and bruising their bark. Gidgerigar and Ooya came running over to the dardurr and begged the women to let them in.

"No," shrieked Gwai-nee-bu above the storm, "there was no kangaroo meat for us; there is no dardurr shelter for you. Ask shelter of the hawks whom you fed."

The men begged to be let in, saying they would hunt again and get kangaroo for the women, not one but many.

"No," again shrieked the women. "You would not even listen to the crying of a little child; it is better such as you should die."

And fiercer raged the storm and louder sang the women:

> Moogaray, Moogaray, May May
> Eehu Eehu, Doon-gara.

So long and so fierce was the storm that the young men must have perished had they not been changed into birds. First they were changed into birds and afterwards into stars in the sky, where they are now, Gidgerigar and Ooya, with the kangaroo between them, still bearing the names that they bore on earth.

COMMENTARY

Culture to the Aborigines means selecting from the full array of natural and psychic energies those that support and maintain collective order and harmony, while rejecting or relegating to ritual those that are disruptive. This legend of the Redbreasts explores the consequences of familiar human interactions and reactions that the Aborigines believed must be carefully restrained or inhibited within the fabric of daily life. Aboriginal social values are distinguished and defined by behavioral norms that contain and transform undesirable human reactions. An example of these sorts of reactions is the drive for personal or individual fulfillment, as depicted first by Gwai-nee-bu and Goomai, who, after killing the hunters's prey, lie about its whereabouts in order to have it to themselves. This greed is reflected back upon them in the action of the hunters Ooya and Gidgerigar, who greedily consume their prey without compassion or concern for the two older women and particularly the young boy.

This behavior conflicts radically with the strict codes of food sharing among Aboriginal kin members in traditional life. These codes are so pronounced that after a hunter has killed and cooked his prey, different parts of the animal are distributed to his various kin, according to directives found in the Dreamtime laws. The hunter might be left with the last morsel—very often the entrails. However, when his nephew or son-in-law makes a catch, he then receives a choice piece of the game.[1] The process of giving, receiving, and belonging to a group is cultivated in Aboriginal society, rather than personal or individual achieving, acquiring, and possessing. This habituation toward sharing and reciprocal exchange is as fundamental to Aboriginal life as buying and selling are in the contemporary world.

The second social value dramatized in this legend relates to child abuse and adult dominance of children. Old Goomai cannot contain her anger with young Gwai-nee-bu, who cries for kangaroo, and her harsh blow to his face draws blood. This type of behavior toward children is absolutely prohibited in traditional Aboriginal culture. Even if a child, in a tantrum, hurls an array of insults or is misbehaving, it is regarded as a severe character flaw for parents, or any other person, to hit or verbally abuse the child. Powerful social structures prevent any form of prohibition or limitation on a child's disposition or activities. The early phase of life is, for each child, a time for openly expressing every drive, emotion, and feeling.[2] It is not until the onset of puberty that children are introduced to laws and disciplines that curb egocentric needs and demands. This behavioral transition, however, is not abrupt, as the children are exposed during the intervening years to an adult society in which there is constant sharing and belonging. The behavioral transition, therefore, is not abrupt.

The Aborigines believe that to violate the innocence of a child interrupts or interferes with the child's spirit taking full possession of his or her growing body. Just as they believe that after death it takes up to three years for the spirit to completely disengage from the physical, so a similar amount of time is needed for the spirit to fully inhabit the body of a young child. Because the Aborigines assure that childhood is a sanctuary of joy, love, and affection, confidence and self-esteem are established early in a child's life. This is often witnessed at around three to four years of age, when young children begin to gain a sense of self, feeling their separateness from their mothers and becoming completely independent in gathering their own food. Similar practices are found among the Amazonian Indians, who also give unlimited affection and freedom to young children.[3] Again there is evidence that unbroken, gentle loving of infants fosters remarkable coordination, confidence, and independence. Visiting the Aboriginal Tiwi people on a remote island off the northern coast of Australia, I joyously watched a group of young children, who with graceful physicality threw themselves onto a foam mat, their twirling, writhing bodies appearing to contort into impossible shapes. Fearful, disciplining adults standing guard over them were conspicuously absent, and youthful laughter and games continued throughout the night, without injury, fighting, or upset.

The third social value raised by this legend of the Redbreasts concerns male-female conflicts in which male physicality is used to dominate women. As our story shows, the women had access to occult powers with which they overthrew the strength and assertiveness of the men. In Aboriginal culture, the imbalance created by male superiority in physical strength and prowess is redressed through an education process in which the male psyche is conditioned and guided by two undeniable laws: that every human being is grown within, and appears from, the womb of a female; and that when life is ended, the body is returned to the womb of the mother earth. These two simple biological facts are symbolic imperatives for the male in recognizing his place in the universal web and for maintaining constant respect for the source of all life, including his own.

In our Aboriginal legend, the two men have undergone initiations into manhood by virtue of being hunters. However, their refusal to share the kangaroo (which the women had actually killed) indicates a lack of respect for the feminine and a naivete about the potency of the archetypal avenging female. Because of this ignorance, the women in this legend, like so many of the female figures in Aboriginal myths, demonstrate and initiate the young men into the hidden powers of the feminine. Through their relentless chanting, they conjure the aid of the winds, rains, and hail. These events exemplify the seemingly limitless powers that emerge from the affinity that women as creators of life have with the universal forces of nature. They trust their ability—not as wirreenuns or witches, but as women—to contact the world of nature spirits.

In Aboriginal tradition, the male initiations act as gateposts through which men pass as they grow in understanding of the mother law and the boundless dynamics of the feminine qualities and forces in nature. The Native Americans, among many other indigenous peoples, honor the feminine as the creator and destroyer of all life. As one Native American man said when asked why the tribal chiefs were elected by women, "Of course the men follow the wishes of the women; they are our mothers."[4]

The limited idea of liberating the feminine within the narrow definitions and theories of the patriarchal worldview is becoming increasingly irrelevant. The feminine ability to convene with the psychic energies that pervade the natural world provides a possible direction for the contemporary feminist movement. Eco-feminism and the upsurgence of the goddess movement approach, in many ways, the reestablishment of nature and the occult as the true sources of feminine empowerment. With the ever-mounting pressures created by environmental destruction, women's goal of assimilating themselves into the male-dominated system will have to shift toward discovering a positive model of femininity, rather than compensating for the wounds and oppressions of the past. It is within the history of Aboriginal and other indigenous cultures that we can explore a societal format and psychological and ethical framework in which the feminine and the earth are held in preeminence.

ENDNOTES

1. Robert Lawlor, *Voices of the First Day: Awakening in the Aboriginal Dreamtime* (Rochester, Vt.: Inner Traditions International, 1991), 165–166.
2. Ibid., 309.
3. Jean Liedloff, *The Continuum Concept* (Reading, Mass.: Addison-Wesley, 1985), 120.
4. C. Gasquoine Hartley, *The Truth about Women* (New York: Dodd, Mead, 1913), 142.

THE WAGTAIL
AND THE RAINBOW

Deereereeree was a widow and
lived in a camp alone with her four little girls.

One day Bibbi came and made a camp not far from hers.
Deereereeree was frightened of him, too frightened to go to
sleep. All night she used to watch his camp, and if she heard
a sound, she would cry aloud, "Deereereeree, wyah, wyah,
Deereereeree."

Sometimes she would be calling out nearly all night.

In the morning Bibbi would come over to her camp and ask
her what was the matter that she had called out so in the night.
She told him that she thought she heard someone walking
about and was afraid, for she was alone with her four little
girls.

He told her she ought not to be afraid with all her children
round her. But night after night she sat up crying, "Wyah,
wyah, Deereereeree, Deereereeree."

At last Bibbi said, "If you are so frightened, marry me and
live in my camp. I will take care of you."

But Deereereeree said she did not want to marry. So night
after night was to be heard her plaintive cry of "Wyah, wyah,
Deereereeree, Deereereeree." And again and again Bibbi
pressed her to share his camp and marry him.

But she always refused. The more she refused, the more he wished to marry her. And he used to wonder how he could persuade her to change her mind.

At last he thought of a plan of surprising her into giving her consent. He set to work and made a beautiful many-colored arch, which, when it was made, he called Yulu-wirree. And he placed it right across the sky, reaching from one side of the earth to the other.

When the rainbow was firmly placed in the sky and showing out in all its brilliancy of many colors, as a roadway from the earth to the stars, Bibbi went into his camp to wait.

When Deereereeree looked up at the sky and saw the wonderful rainbow, she thought something dreadful must be going to happen. She was terribly frightened and called aloud, "Wyah, wyah." In her fear she gathered her children together and fled with them to Bibbi's camp for protection.

Bibbi proudly told her that he had made the rainbow, just to show how strong he was and how safe she would be if she married him. But if she would not, she would see what terrible things he would make to come on earth, not just a harmless and beautiful rainbow across the heavens but things that would burst from the earth and destroy it.

So by working on her mixed feelings of fear of his power and admiration of his skill, Bibbi gained his desire, and Deereereeree married him. And when long afterwards they died, Deereereeree was changed into a little willy-wagtail who may be heard through the stillness of the summer nights, crying her plaintive wail of "Deereereeree, wyah, wyah, Deereereeree."

And Bibbi was changed into the woodpecker, or climbing tree-bird, who is always running up trees as if he wanted to be building other ways to the sky than the famous roadway of his Yulu-wirree, the building of which had won him his wife.

COMMENTARY

The willy-wagtail is a small, black, fantailed bird whose exceptionally spirited, sweet call is heard over vast areas of Australia, making it one of the country's most beloved songbirds.

The swift-flighted wagtail lives, for the most part, in pairs or family groups. In this myth, Deereereeree, the wagtail, uncharacteristically avoids living with a male companion and instead surrounds herself with her four daughters. Again we encounter a Dreamtime situation that is unacceptable in Aboriginal tribal life: a woman living alone, fending for herself and her children. The Australian Aboriginal kinship system was structured in such a way as to allow sexual and family relations to be a natural right for women and men of all ages. Never would a woman be forced to live by herself, nor her children to grow without the support and interrelationship of other men, women, and children. Why does Deereereeree torment herself with loneliness and anxiety and resist Bibbi's advances?

An answer to this question may be found in the symbolically interesting element of the brilliant rainbow, constructed by Bibbi—a colorful pathway that forges a union between the earth and the sky. While the rainbow in this myth is not associated with the Rainbow Serpent found among many Aboriginal tribes, the two images are synchronic in that they represent an energetic or vibratory marriage between the initial polarities of creation: the tangible and intangible, masculine and feminine, sky and earth. The rainbow can be seen as a metaphor for this wedding of opposites by the manner in which it is formed: countless, invisible, ovum-shaped droplets spray from the swelling bellies of clouds to be penetrated by the sun's passionate phallic rays. From this direct union of fire and water, the refracted light unveils a perfect circular arch in which the entire potential of the world of form and color delicately manifests. The rainbow symbolically marks the appearance of the visible from the invisible, the conscious from the unconscious.

In many cultures throughout the world, the rainbow has been associated with a Golden Age or Dreamtime when the forces of the sky and earth, masculine and feminine, were united in harmony. Similar to Bibbi in this story, the Polynesian god Oro fixed a rainbow in the skies, one end forging the heavens, the other resting in a valley on the earth.[1] In Japan, this multicolored bridge of light was also recognized as the roadway of the gods.[2] The Greek goddess Iris was known to travel as a messenger between heaven and earth on the multicolored rainbow.[3] This is only a minute sampling of rainbow images found in many mythologies.

Bibbi's ability to construct a rainbow may be interpreted as proof that he has undergone an initiation in which he experienced the mystery of creation through what the Aborigines refer to as the mother or birthing law.[4] This idea would be consistent with many shamanic cultures in which drums are painted the colors of the rainbow, representing a roadway between the celestial bodies and the earth. As the shamans enter into the depths of the unconscious revelatory realms, the painted rainbow and the constant drumming serve as guides for the inner journey between the two worlds. In all these cultures men return with verification of their sojourn in the pre-manifest realms in the form of magical powers, glistening refractive crystals, or sacred songs.[5]

In this legend, Bibbi verifies his initiatic status by building the colorful pathway in order to impress and win the heart of Deereereeree. Deereereeree's rejection of Bibbi up until this point may represent the fear and inability of a female to fully trust a man and give of herself until he has initiatically experienced the invisible recesses of the Universal Feminine. This interpretation would be consistent with the fact that in Aboriginal life, men have to undergo certain levels of initiation before they are allowed to take a wife.

Bibbi's pronouncements that catastrophic events would "burst" from the earth if the sacred union of male and female, symbolized by the rainbow, was not respected is a warning echoed in many indigenous cultures. These cultures prophesy that if the meaning and rituals associated with the luminous rainbow are lost or defiled, the relationship between men and women, heaven and earth, will disintegrate.[6] Since the Christian era, the sky god of the heavens has gripped religious thought and reverence, while the earth weeps from devastation and exploitation. Perhaps this is an apt warning of the condition of contemporary society, in which uninitiated, power-hungry men control the economic, political, and religious institutions, while the earth, women, and their children become the perennial victims of rape, war, and famine. All of these disasters can be seen as a result of the male-dominant organizations.

Analyzing this myth from a less esoteric point of view, one discovers other layers rich in psychological sophistication. For example, Bibbi seduces Deereereeree, in the words of the storyteller, "by working on her mixed feelings of fear of his power and admiration of his skill." Insights, wisdom, and understanding, as revealed by this statement, abound not only in Aboriginal myths, ceremonies, and worldview but also in indigenous cultures throughout the world. Is it not audacious that contemporary scientists have, under the self-glorifying conceits of evolutionary theory, claimed indigenous culture to be "simple," "savage," and "primitive"? The fact that this legend speaks with relevance to our contemporary crisis, as do countless other ancient Aboriginal legends, indicates yet again the timeless perspicuity of Aboriginal wisdom.

ENDNOTES

1. G. A. Gaskell, *Dictionary of All Scriptures and Myths,* (New York: Avenel Books, 1960), 609.
2. Barbara Walker, *The Woman's Encyclopedia of Myths and Secrets* (San Francisco: Harper & Row, 1983), 840.
3. Ibid., 841.
4. Conversations with Bobby McLeod, Aboriginal singer and activist (August 1992).
5. Holger Kalweit, *Dreamtime & Inner Space—The World of the Shaman* (Boston: Shambala, 1988), 104.
6. Walker, *The Woman's Encyclopedia,* 841.

FOUR

TALES OF HEALING

For traditional Aborigines, illness and death are
considered unnatural: they never occur simply
from biological causes but only as a result of
projected psychic energy through some form of
sorcery. Healing, therefore, requires revealing
the psychic source as well as the cultural or
societal weakness or infraction that prompted
the use of sorcery. With this clarification, the
healer proceeds to clear the psychic distur-
bance as well as administer a physical remedy.
The healed state manifests as a psychic shield
that enables patients to recognize the source of
the illness in their own characters and the
negative projection that they had incurred. In
this way, each person grows in knowledge and
ability to heal his or her own life.

GOONUR,
THE WOMAN-DOCTOR

Goonur was a clever old woman-doctor who lived with her son, Goonur, and his two wives. The wives were Guddah, the red lizard, and Beereeun, the small, prickly lizard. One day the two wives had done something to anger Goonur, their husband, and he gave them both a great beating. After their beating they went away by themselves. They said to each other that they could stand their present life no longer, and yet there was no escape unless they killed their husband. They decided they would do that. But how? That was the question. It must be by cunning.

At last they decided on a plan. They dug a big hole in the sand near the creek, filled it with water, and covered it over with boughs, leaves, and grass.

"Now we will go," they said, "and tell our husband that we have found a big bandicoots' nest."

Back they went to the camp and told Goonur that they had seen a big nest of bandicoots near the creek and that if he sneaked up, he would be able to surprise them and get the lot.

Off went Goonur in great haste. He sneaked up to within a couple of feet of the nest, then gave a spring onto the top of it. Only when he felt the bough top give way with him, and he sank down into the water, did he realize that he had been tricked. It was too late then for him to save himself, for he was drowning and could not escape. His wives had watched the success of their stratagem from a distance. When they were certain that they had effectively disposed of their hated husband, they went back to the camp. Goonur, the mother, soon missed her son and made inquiries of his wives but gained no information from them. Two or three days passed, and yet Goonur, the son, returned not. Seriously alarmed at his long absence without having given her notice of his intention, the mother determined to follow his track. She took up his trail where she had last seen him leave the camp. This she followed until she reached the so-called bandicoots' nest. Here his tracks disappeared, and nowhere could she find a sign of his having returned from this place. She felt in the hole with her yamstick and soon felt that there was something large there in the water. She cut a forked stick and tried to raise the body and get it out, for she felt sure it must be her son. But she could not raise it; stick after stick broke in the effort. At last she cut a midjee stick (from the acacia tree, made with a barbed end) and tried with that, and then she was successful. When she brought out the body, she found it was indeed her son. She dragged his body to an ant bed and watched intently to see if the stings of the ants brought any sign of returning life. Soon her hope was realized, and after a violent twitching of the muscles her son regained consciousness. As soon as he was able to do so, he told her of the trick his wives had played on him.

Goonur, the mother, was furious. "No more shall they have you as husband. You shall live hidden in my dardurr. When we get near the camp, you can get into this long, big comebee [bag], and I will take you in. When you want to go hunting, I will take you from the camp in this comebee, and when we are out of sight, you can get out and hunt as of old."

And thus they managed for some time to keep his return a secret; and little the wives knew that their husband was alive and in his mother's camp. But as day after day Goonur, the mother, returned from hunting loaded with spoils, they began to think she must have help from someone, for surely, they said, no old woman could be so successful in hunting. There was a mystery, they were sure, and they were determined to find it out.

"See," they said, "she goes out alone. She is old, and yet she brings home more than we two do together, and we are young. Today she brought opossums, piggiebillahs, honey, yams, and many things. We got little, yet we went far. We will watch her."

The next time old Goonur went out, carrying her big comebee, the wives watched her.

"Look," they said, "how slowly she goes. She could not climb trees for opossums—she is too old and weak; look how she staggers."

They went cautiously after her and saw that when she was some distance from the camp she put down her comebee. And out of it, to their amazement, stepped Goonur, their husband.

"Ah," they said, "this is her secret. She must have found him, and as she is a great doctor, she was able to bring him to life again. We must wait until she leaves him and then go to him and beg to know where he has been and pretend joy that he is back, or else surely now he is alive again, he will sometime kill us."

Accordingly, when Goonur was alone, the two wives ran to him and said:

"Why, Goonur, our husband, did you leave us? Where have you been all the time that we, your wives, have mourned for you? Long has the time been without you, and we, your wives, have been sad that you came no more to our dardurr."

Goonur, the husband, affected to believe that their sorrow was genuine and that they did not know when they directed him to the bandicoots' nest that it was a trap. Which trap, but for his mother, might have been his grave.

They all went hunting together, and when they had killed enough for food, they returned to the camp. As they came near to the camp, Goonur, the mother, saw them coming and cried out:

"Would you again be tricked by your wives? Did I save you from death only that you might again be killed? I spared them, but I would I had slain them, if again they are to have a chance of killing you, my son. Many are the wiles of women, and another time I might not be able to save you. Let them live if you will it so, my son, but not with you. They tried to lure you to death; you are no longer theirs, mine only now, for did I not bring you back from the dead?"

But Goonur, the husband, said, "In truth did you save me, my mother, and these my wives rejoice that you did. They too, as I was, were deceived by the bandicoots' nest, the work of an enemy yet to be found. See, my mother, do not the looks of love in their eyes and words of love on their lips vouch for their truth? We will be as we have been, my mother, and live again in peace."

And thus craftily did Goonur, the husband, deceive his wives and make them believe he trusted them wholly, while in reality his mind was even then plotting vengeance. In a few days he had his plans ready. Having cut and pointed two stakes, he stuck them firmly in the creek; then he placed two logs on the bank, in front of the sticks, which were underneath the water and invisible. Having made his preparations, he invited his wives to come for a bathe. He said when they reached the creek:

"See those two logs on the bank? You jump in each from one and see which can dive the farthest. I will go first to see you as you come up." And in he jumped, carefully avoiding the pointed stakes. "Right," he called, "all is clear here, jump in."

Then the two wives ran down the bank each to a log and jumped from it. Well had Goonur calculated the distance, for both jumped right on to the stakes placed in the water to catch them, and which stuck firmly into them, holding them under the water.

"Well am I avenged," said Goonur. "No more will my wives lay traps to catch me." And he walked off to the camp.

His mother asked him where his wives were. "They left me," he said, "to get bees' nests."

But as day by day passed and the wives returned not, the old woman began to suspect that her son knew more than he said. She asked him no more, but quietly watched her opportunity when her son was away hunting, and then followed the tracks of the wives. She tracked them to the creek, and as she saw no tracks of their return, she went into the creek, felt about, and there found two bodies fast on the stakes. She managed to get them off and out of the creek; then she determined to try and restore them to life, for she was angry that her son had not told her what he had done but had deceived her as well as his wives. She rubbed the women with some of her medicines, dressed the wounds made by the stakes, and then dragged them both onto the ants' nests and watched their bodies as the ants crawled over them, biting them. She had not long to wait; soon they began to move and come to life again.

As soon as they were restored, Goonur took them back to the camp and said to Goonur, her son, "Now once did I use my knowledge to restore life to you, and again have I used it to restore life to your wives. You are all mine now, and I desire that you live in peace and never more deceive me, or never again shall I use my skill for you."

And they lived for a long while together, and when the Mother Doctor died, there was a beautiful, dazzling bright falling star, followed by a sound as of a sharp clap of thunder, and all the tribes round when they saw and heard this, said: "A great doctor must have died, for that is the sign." And when the wives died, they were taken up to the sky, where they are now known as Gwaibillah, the red star, so called from its bright red color, owing, the legend says, to the red marks left by the stakes on the bodies of the two women, which nothing could efface.

COMMENTARY

The relationship between the Dreamtime legends and the Aboriginal social order is not unlike the relationship we experience between our dreaming and awakened states. When we awake from a dream, we discover the grandeur, horror, ecstasy, or destruction that has taken place and that has expanded the understanding of our inner nature yet has not shattered the relationships and structures of our daily world. That is, our actions in dreams, which can be fulfilling and freeing or devastating and binding, fortunately are not directly transferred to our more stable physical existence. Likewise, the Aborigines know that the power and intensity of the archetypal world cannot be adapted to, or imposed upon, the daily world, except in ceremony. And a large portion of Aboriginal life is given to endless preparation for ever-recurring ceremony.

So in our legend, Dreamtime events and ancestral behavior serve as a guide to what enhances physical life as well as to those things that destroy or retard it. Upon these ancient indicators both cultural and healing practices were laid down. Goonur, the woman-doctor, with her great magical powers heals both her son and his wives and restores harmony to the group; however, judging from her final words, "You are mine now," she has, in doing so, also taken possession of them. In this legend the Aborigines disclose that the relationship between the healer and the healed can become one of co-dependency, or power and possession of one person or group over another.

Contemporary society offers an extreme example of this possibility in people completely surrendering responsibility for their health to a system of drugs and surgery. Our culture provides only the most mechanistic interpretation of our bodies and is devoid of guidance about the body's interaction with mental and psychic processes, as well as the dependency of bodily health upon the "health" of an undisturbed environment. Consequently, we have masses of people dependent on vaccines, drugs, anesthetics, and all sorts of surgical and therapeutical paraphernalia. Our conventional medical system is degenerating into little more than a commercial exploitation of death and disease administered by power- and wealth-hungry medical and pharmaceutical establishments that seek to control or inhibit all other approaches to healing. This is a form of subjugation and possession, which is the shadow side of the archetypal healer-patient relationship. Certain aspects of Western medicine, however, are attempting to emerge from the shadows of control and mass commercialization and are in the process of adopting alternative healing methods. An Aboriginal tribal doctor quoted by A. P. Elkin reveals how Aboriginal methods encourage self-healing rather than a dependency on external means. He said, "I can heal, because I believe my psychic powers are strong enough to enable sick people to believe in themselves."[1]

In the story of Goonur, the wise woman, we can view the complex human interrelationships involved in the process of healing. In one interpretation Goonur can be seen as selfishly restoring life to her son and daughters-in-law and, in repayment, desiring their lives to be lived according to her wishes. In another sense, Goonur symbolically represents the earth or earth mother whom hunting and gathering societies, such as the Aborigines, are indeed possessed by, or indebted to, as the source of all life, nourishment, and healing. This story does not moralize on the evils or dangers inherent in the power of healing; rather, it contemplates the difference between how this power exists in a metaphysical or archetypal context (mother earth) and how the same power can distort or disturb on the level of human psychology.

By maintaining in every ceremony and all aspects of tribal life reference to the ancestral powers infused throughout the creation, the Aborigines avoid falling prey to the psychology of power or possession, whether it be the power to heal, save, or govern. There is no way, in Aboriginal language or societal forms, by which possession or ownership of another person or thing can be expressed or enacted. Also, because of their nomadic lifestyle, there is no motivation to accumulate and possess.

In Aboriginal cosmology the spiritual ancestry of each person is interwoven with the birds, insects, animals, and plants through lineages extending back to the Dreamtime. This worldview is known as totemism. In addition to a hereditary totem, a wirreenun may possess a yunbeai, or animal spirit. This yunbeai, into which a wirreenun has the power to transform in times of danger, is said to be of help in the performance of healing and magic.[2] In our legend it appears that ants are such a totem for Goonur, as demonstrated by the way they come to her aid in resuscitating both her son and his wives. The relationship that exists between an Aboriginal person and his or her totem is symbolic of that person's intimacy with all of the natural world and indicates deep knowledge of all the characteristics and behaviors of even the smallest of animals. K. Langloh Parker points out that even young children know who and what are their totemic families and relations. She relates:

"One day I said to a little Aboriginal girl beside me, 'I wish I could kill all these black ants.'

'Oh . . . ,' said a plaintive little voice, 'they is my 'lations!'" [3]

An Aboriginal person might refer to this legend as "ant dreaming" or "ant language," because it is based on characteristics and potentialities of human life that have been discerned or identified from the observation of ants. We can, in this myth, observe many resemblances, symbolic and physical, between ants and Goonur, the Dreamtime Ancestor. The female ant (queen) builds a small protected cavity in the earth where she will reside in solitary for months, sometimes over a year, caring for her brood of young after they hatch from their eggs.[4] Symbolically, this resonates with the mother earth, who, within herself, gives birth to all of life. Goonur also symbolizes the unconditional equanimity of the earth in that she gives rebirth to her vengeful son as well as his murderous wives.

Like the queen ant, who, without mating again, continues to lay eggs for her long life, Goonur lives to a ripe old age and through her healing continues to be a "birthgiver."[5] As the legend reveals, at the death of Goonur, her fertility or ability to give life through healing is assimilated into the ancestral powers from which it came and, like the stars, will remain as the knowledge of healing is passed from generation to generation.

Ants are a powerful totem for the same biological reason they are known today as the insect superpowers; they inhabit all five continents in numbers never approached by other insects. The given scientific reason for this is their ability to adapt and develop suitable modes of life for the most diverse environmental conditions.[6] Ants have astonishingly precise capacities to pick up and respond immediately to changes in their environment. For example, minute fluctuations in humidity, atmospheric pressure, magnetism, or electricity prior to rainfall are translated immediately into chemical messages that ants pass throughout their population. This shared information results in a flurry of activity in which they may alter various structural and behavioral aspects of their life, including the elaborate passageways of their anthills.[7]

The chemical information that reflects the attunement of insects to the surrounding conditions is transmitted in their venom when they bite a person. Therefore, it is believed that an ant or insect bite can provoke a change in a person's bodily chemistry that allows for a quickening adaptation to a particular place.[8] This acceleration of the communicative relationship between a person and the immediacy of his or her earthly place is a balancing and harmonizing that is necessary for all deep healing to occur and is the form of knowledge Goonur utilizes in this story. Indigenous people in many cultures seek to discover the inherent balance of any natural locale—often they observe that whenever there is a poisonous reptile, plant, or insect present, close by will be an antidote. For example, the painful sting of an Australian bull ant is immediately relieved by the application of the juice of a bracken fern, which typically grows in the vicinity of the ants' nest.

This legend allows us to associate the healing power of insect venom with reestablishing the harmony between characters who have "fallen out of place." The initial imbalance was provoked by the unjustified physical abuse young Goonur imparted on his wives. In this sense, according to Dreamtime law, he was "out of place" in his cultural conduct. His displacement extended to a cycle of revenge, which Goonur the wise woman rectifies by drawing upon a power of the natural world that transcends social morality and personal concerns.

The Maoris of New Zealand, like other indigenous peoples, consider insects, particularly ants, an important and powerful species, and theirs is the first spirit energy they will greet when entering new terrain. The use of stinging ants to revive a person considered dead has also been recorded among a number of indigenous tribes. During Aboriginal shamanistic initiation rituals, masses of stinging ants are used as part of the process of inducing near-death trances.[9] The use of insect venom, most notably that of the tarantula, to achieve mind-altering states has survived within European culture. Tarantula venom has been used as a hallucinatory drug by poets, philosophers, and artists seeking to shed their conditioned mindset and open their consciousness to unknown dimensions. This substance is said to have been used by Rimbaud and Nietzsche and to have inspired the poetic visions of modern American artists such as Bob Dylan and Jim Morrison.[10] Just as the ants' venom in this legend provokes violent twitching in the bodies of the young Goonur and his wives, tarantula venom produces powerful contractions of the cerebrospinal nervous system. Concurrent with these contractions come heightened visual perception and states of emotional and sensory exaltation and intensity, both terrifying and ecstatic. Prolonged use, however, can result in serious degeneration of the central nervous system.[11]

Both the spider and the ant venom have the effect of swiftly altering human consciousness from one level to another. The poets use it to escape the confines of normal consciousness (which to their spirit is deathlike) and achieve ecstatic highs, while in our legend the venom stimulates the flow of life in the limp, drowned bodies of Goonur and his wives. This story (as with so many others we have explored) is a code or parable covertly describing death and rebirth initiatic practices. These forms of ceremony are the profound core and source of Aboriginal spirituality, allowing participants, in trancelike states, to open neural centers within their bodies to communicate with the silent ancestral voices emanating from sacred sites or dreaming places. This death-rebirth experience achieves what is called a healed state through deeper connectivity to both the natural and metaphysical aspects of creation. Illness (seen as a form of spirit possession), ceremonial death, and self-wounding practices are all considered harbingers that periodically call one's energy and vision upward toward the profound and hidden sources of life.[12] Ceremony and healing, therefore, are different aspects of the same body of knowledge.

Within a seemingly simple Dreamtime story we have been able to reflect not only on the use of chemicals derived from insects in ancient healing practices but also on the way psychological, psychic, and metaphysical factors are woven into the Aboriginal knowledge of healing. Many of the newly emerging healing methods are involving this more holistic approach to health. For example, the vanguard of homeopathic practitioners often diagnose a patient's physical ailments by taking into consideration psychic and psychological conditions, including dreams. Homeopathy, like tribal healing, emphasizes the idea of turning inward to stimulate or release natural balancing mechanisms. The remedies administered in homeopathy are produced by a two-phase action of dilution and succussion. Alchemically, dilution is a method of purifying or extracting the essential quality of a substance by reducing it to its most minute quality. This method is opposite to distillation, which extracts a particular quality through concentration. The etymological origin of the word *extraction* is synonymous with the word "ancestry." In other words, when a substance is diluted or distilled to its essence, it resonates with its primal origins or ancestry. The strongest homeopathic remedies are diluted to such an extent that their essence is present not in molecular but only in atomic quantities. The substance has, effectively, been taken back to its atomic ancestry. In this state an exchange of vibratory energy takes place between the source substance and the water in which it is diluted. The molecules of water actually receive a vibratory imprint, a subchemical message from the substance. This highly reduced, yet more energetically potent, message is then "deepened" by a prolonged rhythmic shaking, which constitutes the second phase of homeopathic preparation, called succussion. It is not just energy that is stored in the resulting solution, but also information, and therefore this form of remedy is seen as a direct transfer of information into the body.[13]

An interesting analogy to this two-phase method of preparation can be drawn with the preparation and performance of Aboriginal ceremonies. It may take days, weeks, or even months in preparation for a ceremony. During this time the performers refine their elaborate costumes and body painting. In doing this, they extract the essential quality of their ancestral totem and infuse their identity into that of the archetype. This allows the vital essence of a particular ancestral or animal energy to emerge during the colorful ritual or ceremony. The dancer then begins to pound the earth in rhythm to the clapsticks or didjeereedoo and enter into a repetitive rhythmic movement that may continue for days and nights. This is synonymous with the action of succussion that a homeopathic substance undergoes in order to gain a healing power. Through the vibratory relationship developed from the dancer's feet pounding mother earth, the individual's ancestral imprint and connection with the Dreamtime is deepened. This allows for an energetic transference of knowledge between the dancer and his ancestral spirits and can be seen as analogous to the process of information exchange in homeopathic healing. Entering into ceremony is, in Aboriginal thought, the ultimate healing process.

We can extend this analogy to the legend of Goonur. The bodies of young Goonur and his two wives lie in the water for several days, suggesting the process of dilution. Old Goonur then drags their water-laden bodies to the nearby nest of the stinging ants. As in a successive action, they twitch and shake with the venom of the ants until they are restored to life. This analogy may appear tenuous but becomes less so when one realizes that indigenous hunting and gathering people are aware that each plant is charged with a vibrational spirit energy. It is known that food plants draw up minute quantities of trace minerals, diluting them in their watery tissues; when exposed to the constant rhythmic motion of wind and rain, the mineral energy is potentized in the plant. This energy, derived from and reflective of the particular "place" of a plant's growth, is believed to be imparted to a person who immediately consumes the gathered fruit or plant, and constitutes a healing power in the food. In agricultural societies, where preservation, storage, and transportation are necessary, this healing power is lost.[14]

Plants may have either homeopathic (energetic) or herbal substantive properties. The herbal plants are either of a food or of a ceremonial type— that is, either aphrodisiacs or trance-inducing hallucinogens. Examples of the former are bee pollen and honey, while examples of the latter are ergot from rye grain, and potatoes and tomatoes, which are of the same family (Solanaceae) as the hallucinogens belladonna, datura, and jimson weed.[15] It is interesting to note that when the Inquisitions of Europe suppressed the use of the hallucinogens found in the Solanaceae family, the European population avidly adopted the use of food crops of the same family (tomatoes and potatoes), which had been recently introduced from the New World. It was as if the European population was unconsciously attempting to recapture from these foods a trace of their former spiritual power. As with human consciousness, plants, insects, and animals have the potential to be active in both the work and the play of external life as well as in the mythic dimensions of the inner world. Only with communion (the sacrament of nourishment) between the interdependent realms of nature are these potentials fully realized.

Is it possible to find historical connections between the eighteenth-century system of homeopathic healing developed by German philosopher Dr. Samuel Hahnemann and ancient shamanistic methods, particularly those of women healers? While aspects of Hahnemann's work have been identified by historians as derived from Hippocrates, there is also evidence that he was influenced by his long involvement with the works of the fifteenth-century mystic and alchemist Paracelsus. Paracelsus had formed a major corpus of his writings from having traveled the European countryside during the height of the horrifying Inquisitions. During this heinous episode of European history, spanning five centuries, in which millions of women were tortured and put to death for practicing witch-craft,[16] Paracelsus gathered much vital information on their ancient healing methods. Through the transmission from Paracelsus to Hahnemann, the age-old traditions of women's medicine survived.

Patriarchal Europe paid a heavy price for its destruction and takeover of the healing traditions. The great plagues of Europe spread unchecked in face of the vacuum caused by the destruction of ancient feminine knowl-edge. In spite of this, homeopathic medicine, with its ancestral roots, was used in the cholera plagues in Russia and claimed a mortality of less than 10 percent, in contrast to the mortality rate of orthodox medicine, which reached 60 to 70 percent.[17]

Another interesting connection with the European plagues that is brought to mind through Goonur's story is the relationship between animals and human health. It is now believed that many of the major European plagues resulted from a transfer of organisms from animals to humans through the increased exposure to, and dependency on, domesticated animals such as sheep and cattle. Here the sacred totem relationship between tribal people and animal spirits degenerated into its shadow opposite: mass imprison-ment, exploitation, and slaughter of animals as if they were an empty commodity. That is to say nothing of the defilement and imbalance of this same sacred bond in the destruction of wilderness and wildlife in order to maintain the pastures that feed the "livestock." Evidence is now suggesting that in a related way, AIDS is the result of the transfer of an organism that is harmless in certain species of animals but pathological to human beings. More and more evidence indicates that the oral polio vaccines dispensed to millions of African children in the 1950s contained HIV-like organisms found normally in the kidneys of the tens of thousands of monkeys killed to make the solution in which the vaccine was cultivated.[18] In our igno-rance of the true nature of spirituality and healing, the defilement of the sacred relationship between humans and animals has once again turned into a nightmarish episode of self-destruction.

As in Europe, thin threads of the ancient tradition of women healers have survived the genocide of Christian colonization in Australia. This tradition was being practiced at the turn of the century, and K. Langloh Parker recorded many experiences of her Aboriginal friend Bootha, mentioned in the preface to this book, which, observed by Parker from a European point of view, seemed miraculous.[19]

This same tradition of women's healing is alive today, as witnessed by anthropologist Diane Bell on various occasions. She notes an instance of an Aboriginal man who was brought to women healers and was cured by them when they sang to him the songs and legends of his country. These sung legends, the women told Bell, put the sick man's spirit back in touch with his homeland and with the ancestral powers that had created and continued to sustain his "dreaming place" and therefore his life.[20]

The life-sustaining spiritual relationship between ourselves and our natural habitat, which the Aborigines deem necessary for health, is the very thing we have desecrated and alienated ourselves from. The overwhelming despair, resignation, and terror that arise as we helplessly witness, and participate in, the malignant population explosion and the tormenting rape of the natural world can be healed only if we view it through the ancient eyes of shamanistic cultures. Because our society has denied the need for death-rebirth initiations, the collective unconscious inevitably pushes toward this pattern of destruction in order to be reborn. As we have seen both individually and collectively, Aboriginal society consciously ritualized the universal destructive imperative, and thereby its culture has lived continuously—like a snake simply shedding its skin—for possibly 150,000 years. While we can join Green movements and fight against the corruption and greed of the patriarchal system, a genuine sign alleviating the sense that our civilization is marching undeterred toward a cataclysmic ending is yet to be sighted. Very soon our death-provoking culture must be replaced with one that is life-seeking.

The death-rebirth cycle is the Dreamtime law, a universal triadic code of creation, preservation, and destruction, inbuilt in the childbearing, nursing, and menstrual cycles of women. Therefore, women's roles as birthgivers, nurturers, and healers must be paramount in leading humanity through this crucial transition. The limited rights for women to personally succeed or achieve, obtained through feminism, cannot be seen as an endorsement for remaining under this spiritually famished, solar-focused male system. Although the shudder of fear generated centuries ago by the European witch hunts, as well as continued male domination, has crippling effects on all aspects of the expression of femininity, it may seem that as Western women we have less to fear today. However, the undeterred devouring of the earth's life force in order to feed this deranged consumptive system is perhaps a greater danger than women ever faced before. To be a deeply sensual, or intuitive, expressive, compassionate, or purposeful woman may yet be the most provocative force for change. The questions must now focus not simply on what liberates us, as women, but also on how these freedoms can provoke and serve in a radical transformation of the deep structures of this society.

These Aboriginal legends reveal a social order and a daily ritual life in which women are able to express all of their feminine aspects, both dark and light. Indigenous cultures may be a source from which each of us, in our own way, can accelerate our search for the ceremonies, social forms, medicines, stories, and myths that allow us to dive into the darkest depths and unmask our full array of feminine potentials and power. The mother, the witch; the creator, the destroyer; the bleeding, screaming anger and the compassionate, birth-giving joy; the familiar and comforting as well as the mysterious and abandoned; the persecuted and banished as well as the desired and cherished: the feminine (the holder of balance between life and death) must again be fully present and empowered on earth and in human society so that the inevitable healing ritual of humanity's rebirth can begin.

ENDNOTES

1. As quoted by Robert Lawlor, *Voices of the First Day: Awakening in the Aboriginal Dreamtime* (Rochester, Vt.: Inner Traditions International, 1991), 370.
2. K. Langloh Parker, *The Euahlayi Tribe: A Study of Aboriginal Life in Australia* (London: Constable, 1905), 21.
3. Marcie Muir, *My Bush Book: K. Langloh Parker's 1890's Story of Outback Station Life* (Sydney: Rigby Publishers, 1982), 146.

4. Karl Von Frisch, *Animal Architecture* (New York: Harcourt Brace Jovanovich, 1974), 104.

5. Ibid.

6. Ibid., 106.

7. Ibid., 107.

8. Ibid., 107.

9. Joseph Campbell, *Historical Atlas of the World Mythology,* Vol.1, Part 2, (New York: Harper & Row, 1988), 144.

10. "Highfrontiers," from *Mondo 2,000,* No. 3, 1987, 132.

11. Ibid., 133.

12. K. Langloh Parker, *The Euahlayi Tribe,* 42.

13. Paul Callinan, "Homeopathy: How and Why It Works," from *Simple Living* magazine, Australia, Winter 1989, 18.

14. Conversation with Dr. Grant Lambert, B.Sc. (Hons), Dip. Hom., Dip. Clin Nutr. (October 1992).

15. Michael Harner, *Hallucinogens and Shamanism* (London: Oxford University Press, 1973), 128.

16. Barbara Walker, *The Woman's Encyclopedia of Myths and Secrets* (San Francisco: Harper & Row, 1983), 436–448.

17. Callinan, 20.

18. Louis Pascal, "What Happens When Science Goes Bad. The Corruption of Science and the Origin of AIDS: A Study of Spontaneous Generation," Working Paper No. 9, Science and Technology Analysis Research Programme, New South Wales, Australia: University of Wollongong, December 1991.

19. Parker, *The Euahlayi Tribe,* 42.

20. Diane Bell, *Daughters of the Dreaming* (Melbourne, Australia: McPhee Gribble Publishers, 1983), 154.

THE
BUNBUNDOOLOOEYS

The mother Bunbundoolooey put her child, a little boy, Bunbundoolooey, who could only just crawl, into her goolay. A goolay is a sort of small netted hammock, slung by women on their backs, in which they carry their babies and goods in general. Bunbundoolooey, the pigeon, put her goolay across her back and started out hunting.

When she had gone some distance she came to a clump of dunnia, or wattle trees. At the foot of one of these she saw some large euloomarah, or grubs, which were good to eat. She picked some up and dug with her yam stick round the roots of the tree to get more. She went from tree to tree, getting grubs at every one. That she might gather them all, she put down her goolay and hunted further around.

Soon, in the excitement of her search, she forgot the goolay with the child in it and wandered away. Further and further she went from the dunnia clump, never once thinking of her poor birrahlee (baby). On and still on she went, until at length she reached the far country.

The birrahlee woke up and crawled out of the goolay. First he only crawled about, but soon he grew stronger, and raised himself, and stood by a tree. Then day by day he grew stronger and walked alone, and stronger still he grew, and could run.

Then he grew on into a big boy, and then into a man, and his mother he never saw while he was growing from birrahlee to man.

But in the far country, at last, one day Bunbundoolooey, the mother, remembered the birrahlee she had left.

"Oh," she cried, "I forgot my birrahlee. I left my birrahlee where the dunnias grow in a far country. I must go to my birrahlee. My poor birrahlee! I forgot it. Mad must I have been when I forgot him. My birrahlee! My birrahlee!"

And away went the mother as fast as she could travel back to the dunnia clump in the far country. When she reached the spot she saw the tracks of the birrahlee, first crawling, then standing, then walking, and then running. Bigger and bigger were the tracks she followed, until she saw that they reached a camp. No one was in the camp, but a fire was there, so she waited, and while waiting she looked around. She saw her son had made himself many weapons, and many opossum rugs, which he had painted gaily inside.

Then at last she saw a man coming toward the camp, and she knew he was her birrahlee, grown into a man. As he drew near she ran out to meet him, saying:

"Bunbundoolooey, I am your mother—the mother who forgot you as a birrahlee, and left you. But now I have come to find you, my son. Long was the journey, my son, and your mother was weary, but now that she sees once more her birrahlee, who has grown into a man, she is no longer weary, but glad is her heart, and loud could she sing in her joy. Ah, Bunbundoolooey, my son! Bunbundoolooey, my son!"

And she ran forward with her arms out, as if to embrace him.

But stern was the face of Bunbundoolooey, the son, and no answer did he make with his tongue. But he stooped to the ground and picked therefrom a big stone. This he swiftly threw at his mother, hitting her with such force that she fell dead to the earth.

Then on strode Bunbundoolooey to his camp.

COMMENTARY

In this, our final legend, we are confronted yet again with the absence of clear-cut protagonists, heroes, or heroines and the lack of a defined moral message. Yet, these archaic stories cannot be devoid of this level of meaning, since they are the basis upon which the fundamental social codes, laws, and initiatic knowledge were established and the primary means by which they were transmitted through the generations. Once again, to decipher the subtle multivalent meanings in the story of Bunbundoolooey, I will utilize observations of traditional Aboriginal social values and order as being a living symbol of their worldview and cosmology.

The plot in this legend revolves around the archetypal gesture of a child being deserted by its mother. This structural element also appears in the story of Moses and in the Egyptian myth of the great Mother Isis and her son, Horus, as well as myths from other ancient cultures.[1] The act of abandonment in the Moses story, in which his mother places him in a basket among the reeds, could be seen as a way in which the fundamental societal codes of the Hebraic people, then under persecution and duress, were transmitted to future generations.

Modern women, under the demands and pressures of our society, are often asked to repeat this archetypal pattern of maternal abandonment in order to achieve or maintain economic viability for themselves or their families in a materially motivated world. In socialist and communist societies women were drawn into this same archetypal pattern in order to serve in the work force of the ideal state.

In this Aboriginal legend the maternal act of abandonment is not explained by the preservation or transmission of a culture under threat or by the demands of economic needs, nor is it embellished with socialistic ideals. It is simply Bunbundoolooey's rapacious appetite that compels her to accumulate beyond her means. Bunbundoolooey, overtaken by her obsession to gather more and more grubs, becomes immersed in the excitement of the catch. She moves from tree to tree unaware of and unconcerned by anything else. This compulsion to consume can be compared to the central dynamic of our present competitive society, which is based on a model of unfettered individual drives and ambitions. Theoretically, and often in practice, no limits are placed on legitimately achieving, accumulating, or fulfilling individual ambitions for wealth and power.

Even the word "individual" is utterly misunderstood in our society. "Individual" means a "division," a "fragment," or a "part" and necessitates that this part must belong to a larger whole or entity. However, in the consensual values of our society, the individual is encouraged to behave as if the part were a whole unto itself. Because of this gross misinterpretation, the concept of the individual self functions as a collective, psychological complex.

Competitive commerce thrives upon artificial stimulation of individual ambitions. The marriage of commerce and ambition casts a shadow across the human psyche, which deludes us into believing that our desires, insecurities, and hungers can be fulfilled through unlimited materialistic acquisitiveness. In other words, the "autonomous part" is tricked into believing it can become "whole" by drawing people or things from its surroundings toward or into itself. Today, the validation and exaggeration of individual material goals and ambitions is finally being recognized as the root of antisocial behavior in economically developed Western societies, as well as being unmasked as a major cause of the ever-mounting crime statistics. "Crime is individualism run amok—in corporate suites as well as ghetto streets."[2]

In a sense, we are all conditioned by our society to follow the actions of Bunbundoolooey. The appearance of such behavior in this tragic legend, from a culture that in practice was so removed from egocentric motivation, indicates that the Aborigines fully recognize its presence in human nature and its dangers.

The areas in which the autonomous individual may pursue independence and self-aggrandizement have customarily, in our society, been reserved for men. More recently, women have been invited to engage in this process and these values, often at the expense of their physical health, their emotional well-being, and their genuine responsibilities to society and nature. As well, they are asked to deny the psychic and spiritual development that is particular to the feminine. However, some feminist writers continue to advocate that women should find their freedom by adopting the heroic drives of individualism.

Clarissa Pinkola Estes, for example, equates this same combination of ambition and freedom as a means by which women gain access to what she calls the "wild" feminine state, or the unleashing of the "instinctual self."[3] She ignores, however, that encouraging these same drives in the psyche of men has been directly responsible for the alienation and destruction of the wilderness and the natural world. Estes' work and that of other recent proponents of a "return to the wild" are filtering this primordial human experience through the language and limitations of Western psychology and commerce-based society. Phrases such as "personal pilgrimages" and "deep personal quests" are equated with one's return and reintegration with the "wild," the "earth," and the "natural world."[4] The alleviation of societal oppression and repression that is the hidden side of our individualizing dynamic is a genuine need. However, the obvious contradictions in equating this with a "return to the wild" are not seen by its advocates because, like all of us, they are a product of a social order in which the individualistic complex is blindingly pervasive.

For this reason I recommend that we reach beyond our cultural enclosures by carefully investigating the myths and life patterns of genuinely earth-based cultures. These ancient peoples existed before humanity began its attempts to contain and control the earth. Presently, their cultures, as well as their knowledge of entering into these wild states, are as threatened as the wilderness areas themselves. With the obliteration of the earth's wilderness we also obliterate from the human psyche the potential for freedom, independence, and spiritual integration with the world, as well as the possibility of developing a society that reflects the laws and depth of the wilderness. There remains no better guiding code than the initiatic and social values that prepared indigenous women to live in communication with the conscious, untamed, natural world.

As with the Eastern philosophies that have been adopted by the contemporary Western world, some of the advocates of the "return to the archaic" are grasping only a few elements of the spiritual and shamanistic traditions and are separating them from the society as a whole. The fragmenting of the spiritual element from the fullness of these cultural sources fuels the framework of individualism with its goals of personal enlightenment, personal achievement, and personal salvation.

Personal formal and informal initiations, even within our present alienating society, are still available, since the initiatic patterns—death and rebirth—are inherent in the process of life itself. However, this does not replace the triadic bond between nature, culture, and the psyche that is fundamental to human existence.

One of the most poignant values of indigenous people—one that gives them access to this deep empathetic relationship with the natural world— is perpetuated by women in their mothering role, the very role that Bunbundoolooey deserts. The human infant, because of its lack of physical development, is born into a state of complete dependency, not only on its mother's breasts and body but also on her culture and behavior. An imperative of traditional Aboriginal culture is that the mother fill the void of the child's neediness with a world full of caring, constant affection, generosity, and a deep sense of compassion for all beings. This compassion is conveyed at the moment the infant, in the act of taking food, participates in the inexorable law of earthly existence: the source of one's life is interdependent with the life of everything around one and dependent on the sacrifice or death of others.

> The teaching of compassion begins from the first moment an infant grabs some food or object and brings it to its mouth. The mother or any other relative, usually female, repeatedly uses these moments to plead with the child to share what it has with her. Of course, the mother never takes away what the child possesses or denies it anything it desires, but she finds many opportunities to pretend to be in great need of the infant's generosity. Reinforcing this constant dramatization by the mother is an open society in which people actively share everything with each other. Whenever a weak, ill, or harmless person or creature passes the child's path, the mother fusses over it and showers it with attention, even if it is a scraggly lizard: "Poor thing," the mother declares with great, heartfelt emotion. Food is never denied to anyone or any creature that is hungry. The child experiences a world in which compassion and pity are dramatically directed toward the temporarily less fortunate. The constant maternal dramatization of compassion in the early years orients a child's emotions toward empathy, support, warmth, and generosity.[5]

The Buddha, also, in his discourse on Universal Love, indicated motherhood to be the model on which compassion was based. "As a mother, even at the risk of her own life, protects and loves her child, her only child, so let a man cultivate love without measure toward the whole world, above, and below, and around, unstinted, unmixed with any feeling of differing or opposing interests. . . . This state of mind is the best in the world."[6] It is almost as if Buddha, in turning away from the corruption of his caste-based agricultural society, glanced back to the previous cycle of indigenous cultures from which all civilization emerged. Buddha's doctrine of co-dependent origination, a vision in which humanity lives in an unbroken communicative interchange with the entirety of the physical world, is most probably not a description of a transcendental state of consciousness, yet to be evolved in humanity, but rather a nostalgic remembering and longing for the original perception of the archaic.

In the Aboriginal legend of Bunbundoolooey the young man is void of compassion, reflecting precisely the failure of his mother to convey this emotion to him at that vital stage in his development. He greets the errant mother, who now wishes to reclaim him, by striking her dead with a stone without seeking to understand or question why. The teaching of compassion that Bunbundoolooey fails to enact is vital for the balancing and directing of the necessarily aggressive nature of the masculine toward a more balanced interactive and collective social mode. His action represents the completion of a cycle in which the mother receives retribution for the abandonment of her all-important archetypal role.

Bunbundoolooey's son, therefore, can be seen as the archetype of the present male psyche, which rampantly perpetuates violence, death, and destruction: from the gangs who stalk the streets of Los Angeles, to the clinical scientists tormenting laboratory animals in order to test their chemicals, to each one of us who partake daily of food and busy ourselves with vocations and entertainments while masses of other human beings are starving and tormented. From the insatiable political and corporate manipulators of power, the prerogative to act without compassion in the face of pain, death, and destruction is the footstool of our world order. We are all the incompassionate sons of Bunbundoolooey. When our sense of separateness becomes so pervasive that we do not see ourselves in others or in the world around us, when we exploit the earth as if it were not a living being, we are, in effect, murdering our mother.

Where did the abandonment that set our civilization on this course occur? Many prehistorians are pointing to the Middle East, the birthplace of the spirit of Judeo-Christian society. Here, approximately 3,000 years ago, tribal groups experienced the withdrawal of the earth's all-providing nourishing ground, evidently because of natural hardships and climatic pressures. The Old Testament begins with the story of the loss of a natural environment, a homeland, that had fed these tribal people like a garden. Perhaps the original sin—that is, consciousness gripped by fear and separation—reflects these early people's experience of the loss of the deep sense of belonging to an earthly place—an experience not different from that of a child deserted by its mother.

Is it not symbolically significant that Moses, the prophet of the authoritarian, punishing, and incompassionate God Yahweh, was an abandoned child? This is the concept of God that turned the attention of humanity away from a relationship to the sacredness of the wilderness and the totemic vision of wild animals and creatures to the worship of agriculture, husbandry, masculine-dominated society, and spiritual and social hierarchy and that condoned the extension of power of a chosen people by their colonizing the land of others. This image of the chosen people, later adapted by Christianity and, for that matter, all the colonizing nations is the collective expression of the "chosen" person, the autonomous individual.

> The rule of power and the destruction of the innocent marked the entry of the Hebrews into the Promised Land. When the Hebrews went into Canaan, to claim the land God had promised them, they slew those whom they found there and counted it not among their sins. God says this to Moses about Og, the king of Bashan: "I have delivered him unto thy hand, and all his people and his land. . . . So they smote him and his sons, and all his people until there was none left alive; and they possessed his land."[7]

I would like to return to the Aboriginal legend in order to discover an interpretation of our present situation in this historic cycle. We are, I feel, at a similar stage to Bunbundoolooey's when she is released from the spell of her individual drives and appetites and discovers herself in a land far from her place of belonging. She then has a stark remembrance of her abandoned son. We can interpret this moment on many levels of our present experience, both collectively and individually. Culturally it symbolizes our present need to re-vision the paradigms of our origins and to confront the fundamental premises that are responsible for the atrocities we commit against each other as well as against our precious life source. On a psychological level, it enhances our growing awareness of the full significance of the desertion of our responsibilities toward our progeny, the future generations, which are the only means of our affecting the quality and continuity of human existence on earth.

Many in our society, particularly those with access to psychological and spiritual information, have already, like Bunbundoolooey, turned around and are desperately running back in an attempt to regain what we have lost in the separation from the archaic. However, in awakening from the first obsessional appetite, we are thrown by emotional remorse, fear, and inner needs into what is often a disguised panic.

Bunbundoolooey locates the footsteps of the infant she deserted as they mark his stages of development to maturity. In her deep confusion and anxiety she continues beyond the point where the son's footprints indicate that he has passed the stage of adolescence. It is possible at this moment for Bunbundoolooey to recall that the profound loss was not of her physical child but of her revelatory cultural laws, which insist not only on a deep and constant intimacy between mother and infant but also on the "conscious abandonment" of her maternal role as the boy enters his adolescent initiation. This remembrance could force her to stop and confront her loss, deep grief, and guilt on an inner level, allowing her to transform this death and despair into an initiatic rebirth for herself.

Instead she plunges on to face and even try to reclaim her transgression on its physical manifestation, the incompassionate alienated man/son— and he slays her. This, perhaps, is the choice left to us now, to recognize the deep metaphysical laws whose vague outlines are still imprinted in what remains of indigenous myths and culture and accept that this cycle requires us to reimagine the rebirth from the beginning. Or, if we ignore this option, as is the case in much of society (both "New Age" and "mainstream"), we are left with an attempt to pull the archaic vision into our present structure, ignoring the disturbed and distorted relationship between psyche, society, and the earth upon which these structures are based.

This Aboriginal legend is not a fatalistic prophesy. Rather, like all the other forms of Aboriginal ritual culture, it reveals a wide spectrum of human possibilities. I believe that the choice rejected by Bunbundoolooey is where the healing lies for our contemporary dilemma. Through the compassionate, birth-giving consciousness of the feminine, we as women have the innate courage and love of life to comprehend its source and forgive, or at least accept, the historical deviation that has led to our contemporary crisis. In order to do this, we must remove the image of ourselves as victim and in healing our wounds regard them as our initiation and preparation for the struggles ahead.

These archaic legends offer us a glimpse of the unlimited power of the primal feminine to create and regenerate life. The translations of these myths and their fidelity to the Aboriginal sources was the work of a childless woman, K. Langloh Parker. Perhaps because her life was saved by an Aboriginal girl, she directed her natural mothering instincts toward birthing these legends into contemporary awareness. The legends form a link in a chain that connects us to the power and strength of the traditional Aboriginal women, who, in Langloh Parker's time and even now, carry forth, under the most trying circumstances of cultural and spiritual disillusionment, the essence of this most ancient sense of reality.

ENDNOTES

1. *Encyclopaedia Britannica*, 11th ed., vol. 28 (Cambridge: Cambridge University Press, 1911), 895.
2. Charles Derber, "A Nation Gone Wild," *Utne Reader* March/April 1993, 67 (Excerpt from *Money, Murder and the American Dream: Wilding from Wall Street to Main Street* (Winchester, Mass.: Faber & Faber, 1992).
3. Sara Rajan, *Civilizing the Wolf* (Santa Cruz, Calif.: Unpublished, 1993), 2.
4. *The Box: Remembering the Gift* (Santa Fe: Terma Company, 1993).
5. Robert Lawlor, *Voices of the First Day: Awakening in the Aboriginal Dreamtime* (Rochester, Vt.,: Inner Traditions International, 1991), 247.
6. Barbara Walker, *The Women's Encyclopedia of Myths and Secrets* (San Francisco: Harper & Row, 1983), 694.
7. Andrew Bard Schmookler, *The Parable of the Tribes* (Boston, Houghton Mifflin, 1986), 46.

BIBLIOGRAPHY

All the legends were selected from these three books:

Parker, K. Langloh. *Australian Legendary Tales: Folklore of the Noongahburrahs as Told to the Piccannies.* Collected by Mrs. K. Langloh Parker. Introduction by Andrew Lang. London: David Nutt: Melbourne: Melville, Mullen & Slade, 1898.

> The Rainbird
> The Redbreasts
> The Wagtail and the Rainbow
> Goonur, the Woman-Doctor
> The Bunbundoolooeys

———. *More Australian Legendary Tales.* Collected from various tribes by Mrs. K. Langloh Parker. London: David Nutt: Melbourne: Melville, Mullen and Slade, 1896.

> Sturt's Desert Pea, the Blood Flower
> Where the Frost Comes From
> Bralgah, the Dancing Bird
> Piggiebillah, the Porcupine

———. *Woggheeguy: Australian Aboriginal Legends.* Collected by Catherine Stow [i.e., Mrs. K. Langloh Parker]. Adelaide: Hassell, 1918.

> Wahwee and Nerida: The Water Monster and the Water Lily
> Dinewan the Man Changes to Dinewan the Emu
> Murgah Muggui, the Spider
> Moodoobahngul, the Widow
> The Wirreenum Woman and Her Wirreenum Son